F*#k

THE DOUBLE STANDARD IN DATING

HEATHER JONES

This book is dedicated to my mom, and life-long best friends Genice Abshire, Stephanie Davis, Christie Thomason, and Kate Good. Thank you for your unwavering support and belief in me— and for keeping all my dirty secrets safe. ☺

~

This book is also dedicated to my Daddy, who recently passed away. He always wanted to write a book about his life—I'd be his ghost writer. Though we talked and talked about it, I never actually pushed him to put pen to paper. Now I wish I had. Along with his writing dream, his unique voice is lost.

While I can't recover his story in his words, his memory and influence lives on with me. And I know he's proud of me for not letting go of my dream. It's been a long time coming.

Introduction

I don't know about you, but growing up I was taught dating was just a means to an end—with the end being marriage. We were supposed to put ourselves out there and hope for the best, waiting for the day we'd meet "the one" and our lives would suddenly fall into place. Well, my experience hasn't been quite like that, and I'm guessing yours hasn't, either.

Year after year, I kept dating with marriage in mind, and year after year kept running into the same brick walls. Several years ago—after yet another failed attempt at a relationship—I decided to start documenting my dating experiences. After some time, I noticed there was one common brick in every single wall: me.

I finally admitted it was time to look within to see what I was doing wrong. It didn't take long for some patterns to emerge—the same mistakes being made over and over and over again. For example, I'd meet a guy and immediately think he was *the one* and throw my heart into the relationship, only to have it broken a few weeks or months later. Or, I'd try to force the relationship to work even when I knew the guy wasn't *the one* and ultimately end up getting hurt or hurting him. Or, at my worst times, I'd quickly move from one guy to another hoping one would eventually be *the one*, taking it personally and damaging my self-esteem with each relationship that didn't work out. I was dating like a wind-up doll in a 4x4 brick cell.

But imprisonment does at least aid introspection. I thought long and hard about marriage. I was well into my 30s by this time, and I knew I had to ask myself some tough questions like, "What if I never actually find the one?" "What if I don't get married?" "What if I never have kids?" "Would it be so bad if I didn't get married or have kids?" "What would my family think?" "Is it bad I like being single?" "Is there a reason I'm not married?" "Is there something wrong with me?" In this state of hyper paranoia (I mean, thoughtful self-examination), I finally admitted to myself I had no business being married. And, to my surprise, I felt…peace. I suddenly accepted the fact marriage might never happen for me, and I was actually more than fine with it (try having that conversation with your mother).

So how does one move forward, break the husband hunting habit, still date, and have fun? Good question. I had no idea either.

I'd been husband hunting for so long I had no clue how to just "date." But, I had to start somewhere. I began venturing out by myself or with friends for any and every occasion, and I went on dates. A LOT of dates. Sure, I continued to make the same mistakes I mentioned earlier, and trust me, the transition was not easy as you'll soon find out. Over time though, I got to know myself better, and the mistakes lessened. I began to understand the ins and outs of what I now refer to as "casual dating." And, best of all, I was having fun doing it.

I soon realized casual dating gives you the chance to figure out what you do and don't like about various types of men, and what you will and won't tolerate from them. You learn how to set boundaries with yourself and others. With no strings attached, you can date outside your comfort zone, end relationships when the time is right rather than dragging them out to a painful end, and have a good time without getting hurt or hurting someone else. When approached from a place of discovery instead of desperation— when things are kept *casual*—dating is not only fun, it builds rather than breaks your self-confidence and self-esteem.

Essentially, I had learned to date like a man.

Which brings me to one double standard: When a man meets a woman, he's not wondering, "Is she stable?" "Will she cheat on me?" "How does her name sound with mine?" "Will she make a good mother?" or "Could I marry her?" No! He's thinking, "I wonder if she's wearing panties." "Is she a cool girl?" "Will she come home with me tonight?" "Those are nice lips." and "Are those real?" Women analyze and overthink every poor guy to death before he even has a chance to order dessert. Men enjoy women and don't make a big deal about it. It's time for women to do the same.

So how did this double standard come about? GUILT. It's that nasty emotion women are way more susceptible to than men. When a man dates a woman, sleeps with her, enjoys her for a while and moves on, he's not thinking about the long-term impacts on her self-esteem. Nor should he. It's really up to the woman to decide what she's cool with and not cool with, and act accordingly. Women should view men the same way. If a girl wants to sleep with a guy for the fun of it, she should do it. Most guys know what they're getting into, and it's not up to the girl to worry about how it's going to affect him. If she "tries out" a guy with a few dates and isn't having fun, there's no harm in moving on. In fact, as this book will explain, there's probably less harm in the long run. Women need to learn to enjoy men (and not feel guilty about it).

I know. I know. It's much easier said than done. Most girls are not raised this way. As I mentioned, many of us are raised to believe our end goal should be marriage (and two kids, two dogs, and a white picket fence). We're also raised to care about others' feelings, act "proper," and feel guilty or ashamed when we don't. Ultimately, we're raised to act as though we'd make a good wife. When guys don't follow these same rules, we get hurt. All of this makes for a very uneven 'dating' field. Well, I'm here to help even things out.

This book is not a guide to help you find Mr. Right. It's a book to help you find you, because when it comes to men, we often lose who we are very quickly. We think we're carefully stepping into the shallow end of the pool, only to quickly find ourselves drowning at the bottom of the deep end. My goal is to keep your head above water.

In the pages that follow, you'll find hundreds of awesome tips to help you navigate through the world of casual dating. These tips are designed to help rewire the way you think, learn to be in the moment, and *enjoy* dating, rather than waste time wondering how good your date will look standing at the altar.

Everything you're going to read in this book is absolutely one-hundred-percent factual and true. I've not embellished any details to make the stories more entertaining, so don't go judging me as you flip through these pages. I'm putting all of my own real experiences out there, and I'm pissing off a bunch of dudes by doing it. So be kind, learn, and grow from what I share with you. I really do want to help you understand all aspects of casual dating (good and bad) so you can truly enjoy and make the most of each-and-every experience.

We'll chat about what a "casual" relationship is and how long it's supposed to last. I'll give you tips and tricks to get through each "stage" of a casual relationship. You'll find scenarios or examples for almost every dating situation imaginable. You'll learn how to keep from falling for the wrong guy, when to get out, how to spot the guys who are just out for a good time, and, more importantly, how to stay in control of yourself because "Control is Key"—a line I take with me everywhere I go.

So where am I now? I'm happily single. I have amazing friends, a lot of fun, and no regrets! I can't say for sure I'll casually date forever, but why should I settle just to say I'm settled down?

As I mentioned earlier, my transition didn't happen overnight. I cried myself to sleep many nights along the way—still do from time to time. My wish is to help minimize the tearful nights in your life, so you can get to the fun faster.

It's time to start a dating revolution ladies! F*#k The Double Standard in Dating!

With love,
Heather

Table of Contents

The Double Standard in Dating

Over the course of the last few years when asked by any guy what my book is about, I've said, "It's a book about casually dating. I teach women how to casually date with no strings attached." This comment is invariably responded to with something like, "Oh that's so cool!" "I love that!" "Women need that!" The conversation typically makes its way to the topic of sex, and the guy suddenly stops to think for a second. He realizes he just applauded me for teaching women how to casually date, but also realizes it probably means these women are sleeping around. Let the back pedaling begin. Fast.

At this point the conversation gets deep. We talk social stigmas—how what's acceptable for guys is not acceptable for girls. Men are praised for dating multiple women and sleeping around, but women are shamed. We move on to discussing society's current state of affairs. The fact is women are waiting much longer to get married or have children. Many women today are very focused on their careers, and they don't have to rely on a man for security. It's hard to deny in today's day and age of worldwide educated, successful, independent, single women, with huge bank accounts, excellent credit scores, home ownership, executive gym memberships, and drawers full of sex toys, men are slowly becoming obsolete in the traditional sense. And, it absolutely scares the living shit out of them. "Oh, that's cool," quickly changes to "I need another drink."

Let's be honest. Women have been dating multiple men for a long time now—but no one talks about it. Why? Because guys really can't handle knowing they aren't the only one you're dating. And once they find out...you'll get branded as being a "slut," right? Even if you're just *dating* multiple men, it's assumed you're having sex with them all. Why? Because society deems it normal for two people who are dating to have sex within a few dates—and most men won't continue casually dating a woman for long unless there's sex involved.

Here we have arrived at The Double Standard in Dating.

Guys like the idea of a woman who is fun, has no drama, is successful, and does her own thing. But once they realize you're out there having fun (and likely having sex) with a few other guys, too, it gets tricky.

Listen, I'm in no way, shape, or form telling you to go out and sleep around. Sex is a very personal decision only you can make, and only you will know how it makes you feel. You can successfully date more than one guy at a time without sex being involved—it just takes practice. Or, have sex with one or all the guys you're dating if you want to. Who cares? Women have long had to play by one set of rules, while guys have gotten to play by another. It's time to change the rules of the game, and I'm here to coach you through it.

The Prelude

2

The Prelude

Before we get started, I think it might be helpful for you to see how bad things got for me before they got better. At times, the advice I give isn't going to be easy to follow. You may question whether you're cut out for casual dating, whether you have enough confidence for it or ever will. Perhaps you're worried I don't really understand just how bad men can mess with your head. Or worse, maybe you're worried I'd judge you for doing something crazy. Well…the following story should ease your mind. One, you'll understand I could never judge any behavior a woman's resorted to because a man caused her reason to take a vacation. And, two, you'll see if I can conquer casual dating after what happened to me, anyone can.

Before I started documenting all my dating experiences, I was in a very serious long-term relationship I thought would last forever. I was so in love (and three-bridal-magazine-subscriptions committed to getting married) I didn't want to admit to myself (or anyone else) I wasn't actually ready. Thankfully, my boyfriend saw in me what I didn't see in myself, and we were able to part ways as friends.

About two months after our relationship ended, I made the first attempt at rewiring my dating mentality. Instead of thinking about a date as a husband-hunting adventure, I decided to strip it down to what it really was: two people getting together to have fun with no need to mentally fast forward to our wedding day. I thought I had the right frame of mind. I felt strong, confident, and ready to get out and have fun. I was destined for dating success. But that was clearly not the case.

> **Translation:** I fell hard for the first guy I had a real attraction to. ***Dating mistake number 1:*** *Allowing a meet up for drinks to turn into a two-week, non-stop soiree right after a serious breakup*

The Prelude was passionate, successful, and very good at finessing women. He was super funny (always a clincher for me), liked to have fun, allowed me to be myself, always complimented me, and always couldn't wait to see me again. He made me feel special. And, he was a "bad boy." (I love bad boys…always have).

I had put it out there to my friends I was interested in meeting new people and ended up getting The

6

Prelude's number from one of them. I gave him a call to introduce myself, and we decided to meet at a bar for drinks. The attraction was instant (at least for me it was). He was nice looking and a little conservative, but made me laugh like crazy. What got me most though, I have to admit, was the cocky air about him. He was a jerk to everyone else but me, and I loved it. I felt protected, excited, and giddy—within the first five minutes. As I said before, The Prelude was the kind of guy who knew women really well— and knew how to play them. He immediately saw my weaknesses and used them to his advantage. (Yes, guys do this. A lot.) He could tell I was fresh out of a relationship and hungry for a connection. He wasted no time providing one for me.

That night we also found a common bond—both of us liked to "party." So…the party began, and we literally stayed up for days talking, laughing, and having lots of sex. I couldn't get enough of him, and he seemed to feel the same. I told him all my dreams and fears; he told me his. I thought I had found the one, again.

> **Translation:** Drugs and/or alcohol can intensify feelings that aren't necessarily real. ***Dating mistake number 2:*** *Mixing partying with dating early on*

Within two weeks The Prelude took me to a wedding in his hometown (out of state), where I met his friends and family. We went to several events and parties, and I got the "looks and nods" of approval. Also during this weekend, we shared a very intimate moment. We had been partying of course, and I got super sick. He stayed up all night taking care of me, which only made me fall for him more. He was super caring and very gentle…a side of him I really hadn't seen yet. I distinctly remember him holding me in the bathroom and saying "Goddammit, Heather, I did not want to feel this way about you!" I took his comment to mean he had fallen for me, which made me feel so much better because I had certainly fallen for him. Such an experience, you'll find out later in the book, can make or break a relationship.

After we got home, we spent the next three weeks together, every day and every night. I could not believe I had met someone so perfect for me so quickly after my last relationship. Based on his actions, I assumed he was interested in having a lasting, serious relationship with me, which only made me want to give more of myself to him.

Translation: A guy will often give you the subtle impression he wants something serious, when actually he doesn't. Why? To avoid confrontation and have unlimited access to sex. That is, until he decides it's getting too serious. ***Dating mistake number 3:*** *Assuming that meeting friends and family, spending every waking moment together, and sharing an intimate moment means a guy wants a serious relationship with you*

I left his house for work one Friday morning, and he said, "I'll see you tonight." Excited about our upcoming weekend, I called him later that afternoon to see what the plans were. He never called me back. In fact, he never called me again.

Of course, I continued to call him incessantly. He sent my calls directly to voice mail and wouldn't return any of my messages.

Translation: If he isn't communicating with you, he's done with you. ***Dating mistake number 4:*** *Refusing to move on when it's so painfully obvious the guy already has*

Sound familiar? Anyone? As I'm sure you can imagine, I quickly went from being "in love" to being OBSESSED.

I went nuts thinking of all the different things he was doing, all the women he was probably having sex with, all the fun he was having without me. I tried to figure out what I had done. What mistakes did I make that drove him away? What was wrong with me? I analyzed every detail of our time together. I listened to the songs that reminded me of him over and over again. I called him even though he wasn't calling me back. I made my friends go with me to places where I thought he'd be, did drive-bys of his apartment, called his friends, and cried myself to sleep alone watching re-runs of Sex in the City every night for what seemed like forever. I went from love to obsession in the time it takes Danica Patrick to do a lap.

Weeks later, he finally called, and of course, I answered immediately. He acted like nothing ever happened, so I pretended like I was fine, like no time had passed, like I was totally okay. He said he couldn't wait to see me, and I fell for it. I was right back to jumping at the chance to see him every time he asked. But it only lasted for a couple of weeks before he cut off communication again, and I quickly reverted to obsessed stalker again, trying to "run into" him, driving by his house, and stopping by to entice him with sex, as if he'd suddenly realize how much he missed me and want to be with me forever.

Translation: A desperate woman is never attractive to a man. ***Dating mistake number 5:*** *Not having enough self-respect to walk away from a bad situation*

I finally started to get the hint and stopped my restraining order-inducing behaviors. Well, all except for one more itty-bitty incident…

After about a month had gone by with little or no communication, he, of course, called. It was 9 a.m. on a Sunday, and he was in the Bahamas on a family trip. Just like last time, he said he couldn't wait to talk to me and that he really missed me. He had to see me that night when he got home. And, again, I was excited. I thought, "Wow, he's calling me first thing in the morning while he's on a family trip in the Bahamas. He must have been thinking about me. He must have finally realized how much he wants to be with me." (Unless you've never lost all better judgment when dealing with a man, in which case you probably wouldn't be reading this book, no rolling your eyes.)

I was leaving for Denver that night, so I told him I'd love to see him when I got back. He begged me not to go, said he really wanted to see me and spend time with me. He said he couldn't wait until I got back from Denver. I was so hopeful this meant we were really going to be together forever this time I ended up postponing my trip until the next day. He called me on his layover in Miami just to check in and let me know he'd see me around 9:30 p.m. When he hadn't called by 9:30, then 9:45, 9:50, 9:55, I started to get a little anxious.

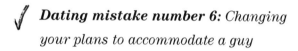 ***Dating mistake number 6:*** *Changing your plans to accommodate a guy*

At approximately 10:00, I lost my ever-lovin' mind. I'm not talking a momentary lapse of reason here, girls. I'm talking full-on, wild-eyed, crazy *Fatal Attraction* shit.

I made the normally 45-minute drive to the gated entrance of his apartment community in 20 minutes flat. With no remote, no code, and no answer to my 17 calls to him, I did what any other temporarily insane girl would do: I waited for someone else to come home and gunned it through the gate behind them.

Dating mistake number 7: *Letting emotions take control of your actions*

His car was parked in its spot, and I could see through the peephole the lights and TV were on in his apartment. I knocked on the door—no answer. I knocked again. Then I pounded. I continued for more than five—okay, ten—minutes. No answer. The next natural thing to do, of course, was to walk around the side of the building, in my heels, in the dark, in sprinkling rain, through dirt and grass, to peer up several stories into his windows. (Stop judging—like you've never done anything like this.)

What happened next is a bit of a blur, but it went something like this...

I saw the lights on in his bedroom and thought I heard and saw him having crazy sex. Then it happened...I lost any remaining shred of reason I had. I looked down, saw my keys in my hand, and threw them at the window as hard as I could. When they landed in the dirt in front of me, I picked them up and did it again. And again. And again.

I was crying and saying things a sweet Southern girl should never say, much less shout, at 11 p.m., on a Sunday, outside, for a whole neighborhood to hear.

He came to the window, only "he" wasn't The Prelude. This guy had bleached blonde, spiked hair. In my insane fog, I guess I had misjudged floors and threw my keys at the wrong window! Four times!

What took place next could've seriously been sent in for an episode of COPS. My keys had fallen into the bushes. It was dark and the sprinkles had turned to rain. My heart was racing, and I thought I was having a panic attack. I tried to dig through the bushes to find my keys, but they were buried too deep.

Then to my right, I heard a noise. The half-naked blonde guy was coming straight toward me. I took off around the other side of the building toward the parking lot, staying low behind bushes until I got to my car. I tried the back door handle, and thankfully, it opened. I crouched down on the floorboard in the back and called Kate, my roommate, to come get me.

Lying there, all I could think about was how stupid I'd been. I prayed to God The Prelude hadn't seen me. After 45 minutes, my roommate pulled up. When I snuck out of the backseat, I looked across the parking lot and saw the blonde guy was still walking around the cars. He spotted me and started running toward us—with a gun!

I heard him shout "Heather!" but I ran to Kate's car anyway. I jumped in, and she hit the gas. When I looked back, Blondie had turned around and was running the opposite way to head us off at the entrance. I was thinking, "How does he know my name?" And gun and all, I still thought, "What if The Prelude found out what happened and that's how he knows my name?" I was that pathetic.

As we pulled out of the exit gate, the man ran in front of our car. Kate slammed on the breaks. The guy was armed and clearly pissed. Fear was quickly overtaking my insanity, and I was starting to—yes, finally—see things had gone too far. I was not sure what to do at this point.

I decided to get out of the car and face the situation. Blondie was out of breath. He was yelling, calling me an f'ing bitch (among other things), and waving the gun around. "What the f were you doing?" he yelled. "Why did you disturb me and my wife? Are you f'ing crazy?"

As I tried to calm him down and explain what happened, his wife ran up behind him. I was still trying to explain. I said I thought he was someone else. I began to try to explain the whole story—the relationship, the unreturned calls, the toying with me—until Blondie's wife finally said, "What the f is wrong with you? Don't you have any self-respect?"

I was humiliated and just wanted to leave, but evidently I had cracked their window with my keys. And, as luck would have it, they knew The Prelude and threatened to tell him the whole story if I didn't give them money right there on the spot to pay for it. Thankfully, Kate had $100 cash on her, which pacified them enough to let us leave.

The next morning I was exhausted from crying all night, but I had to find my keys and get my car. Kate drove me back to his house…the worst drive ever. I was on the verge of throwing up the whole time. I had postponed my trip and now would likely miss my flight because I had to deal with all this. I found my keys. They, along with the "Heather" keychain I had bought in Florida, were hanging on a branch of a bush below Blondie's window. Guess that's how he knew my name.

I was hoping to get out of there without seeing anyone (especially Blondie or Blondie's wife). The Prelude was usually working at this time, but as I was driving out of the apartment community, you guessed it, he was driving in. Despite all that happened the night before, seeing him flipped my insanity switch. Again. I turned around and drove back to his apartment. He saw me coming but ignored me. He walked into his apartment and closed the door. I went up and knocked. Surprisingly, he let me in. I could not control my emotions at this point and let him have it. "How could you do this to me?" I screamed. "I postponed my trip to be with you. What happened to you last night? Why didn't you call me?"

"I fell asleep," he said. That was it. No further explanation.

Believe it or not, I continued to see The Prelude for a few months after this. That is, of course, whenever he decided to call. I was that desperate to be with him. Well, I was just plain desperate. Period. I continued to let him degrade me, use me, and toss me to the side when he was finished.

> **Dating mistake number 8** *(and what all the other mistakes come down to): Dating without any shred of dignity*

So what's the moral of this story? That any woman— and I mean any woman, no matter how self-assured, strong, attractive, and successful she is—can lose her mind over a guy. It doesn't make her a bad person. It doesn't even make her crazy. It makes her human.

You've read in this story a few (very common) dating

mistakes women make. Everyone makes mistakes. But not learning from them is the biggest mistake of all. Some of you might be thinking what an asshole The Prelude was. But that's not what I'm here to talk about. Boys will be boys. It's how we deal with them that makes the difference.

Clearly, as you now know, my entry into casually dating was not easy. But even I finally learned from my dating mistakes. And if I can, you can to. I promise. It *is* possible to rewire the way you think about dating. It *is* possible to recognize when a relationship is supposed to be casual and nothing more. It *is* possible to enjoy those casual relationships. It *is* possible to stay in control and have fun doing it. And, perhaps most importantly, it *is* possible to retain your self-respect while casually dating. So, let's begin.

3

Casual Dating Playbook

I like to think of casual dating like coaching a baseball team. I build a bench, secure a few star players, and never forget my cheering friends. Fundamental rules must be followed for every stage of the game, or no one has fun. The games should begin and end with excitement. There will be good plays, bad plays, celebrations, and possibly an injury or two. But all should leave the field knowing they had fun.

Think of this section as the playbook for successful casual dating. Commit these tips and rules to memory—they apply to any phase of dating. Then, play ball!

Practice makes perfect. Casual dating gives you the perfect opportunity to learn about yourself and about men. It's okay to make mistakes, get your heart broken, and break some hearts. But always learn the lesson and move on. With practice, you'll soon be a fun, confident woman having a blast.

The Bench. I have to give my girlfriend Kate the credit for coining this term as it sums up so well my whole dating philosophy. Absolutely, under no circumstances, should you date one guy at a time. Have a "bench" of guys, and always keep it fresh with new recruits. You can, of course, have your star players, but keep your eye on the ball. You're just having fun. Also, having a bench doesn't mean you should deceive any of the men on it. It does, however, mean you should never focus on just one. I cannot stress the importance of this tip enough. It took me a long time to embrace this philosophy because I felt guilty for running around with a few different guys. It was The Dating Double Standard hammered into my brain that prevented me from understanding dating more than one guy at a time was actually the key to my salvation. Don't worry…we will explore more of this throughout the book.

Build the bench. I don't claim to be an expert on how to meet men, but I will give you one tip. When I started out, I approached dating much like I approached learning how to country dance. The only way to learn was to practice, and the only way to practice was to say yes to whoever asked me to dance. At first I tripped all over my feet, looked like a fool, and ended up on my butt once or twice. But now I can two-step and swing dance like a pro. You might go on lots of first dates. That's okay. The point is to get out there. Who cares if you get your toes stepped on a few times?

Keep your eye on other leagues. Not only do you want to build your bench locally, you want to build it nationally and internationally. It's great to date guys who live in other cities and countries. One, you don't have to worry about running into them when you're out with another dude. Two, you get to have all the fun that comes along with weekend getaways every time you see each other. Three, you prolong the life of the relationship without it getting serious. Four, you get to travel outside your city on a regular basis. Five, you don't have some guy up your ass all the time wondering what you're up to because he's back in his city dating around, too. Six, it doesn't matter if you don't see him every few months—actually, you both prefer it that way. Seven, you always look forward to the next time you get to see him—whenever that may be. Eight, it's easier to end these types of relationships—you just stop calling or texting each other. Shall I go on?

Have at least one well-rounded player on your bench at all times. Going to a destination wedding alone can be a bummer. So, it's good to have at least one guy on your bench who will likely never be an all-star, but you'll probably be friends forever. He's "safe." The heat stays on simmer between you, and he harbors no potential for embarrassing you or anyone else, even when the chicken dance comes on. Plus, when you're at this type of event with a guy you're super attracted to, there's a strong possibility you'll be out on the floor dancing to some sappy shit song, gazing up at him, and thinking how good of a dancer he is, how nice it feels to be in someone's arms, how good he looks in a tux, etc. Then you get all the people there telling you how cute you two look together, blah, blah, blah. Suddenly you're drinking way too much champagne and leaping toward the flying bouquet.

Know your players' positions. While you're out there dating for fun, you need different categories of men: ideal dinner dates, great movie partners, fancy event escorts, hiking buddies, Sunday Fun-day friends, Saturday night booty calls, etc. It's important to find several guys, rather than one, to fulfill your needs and fit the various parts of your life.

Always have a pinch hitter. The worst thing in the world is finding yourself sitting at home alone on a Saturday night when you thought you had plans with someone. Therefore, a bench full of subs and a backup plan is a must for casual daters. Whether you go out with another guy or with your girlfriends, never sit at home stewing about what could have been. Send in a sub, and it will likely turn out to be the best night you've had in a long time.

Make good trades. Increase your standards with each new guy. The next one should always be nicer, more polite, more stable, more attentive, a better communicator, better in bed—better on all levels than the last guy was. Why digress? The more secure you become in casual dating, the more confidence you'll exude, which you'll need the next time you want to test the waters with a guy you never thought you could have.

Once a guy's made the team, stop making him prove he deserves to be on it. When you're casually dating (or any kind of dating for that matter), it's not cool to give a guy a test. You know what I mean… maybe you toss out a scenario to see how he reacts or put him in a situation on purpose to see what he does. Another great one is to make up an emergency to see if he drops everything to help you. Number one: A guy knows when you're testing him, so don't even try it. Number two: if you feel like you have to test a guy, then you're not casually dating. You're trying to trick him into a relationship. He'll be seeking a trade to another team in no time.

"Reputable" players have their reputation for a reason. If a guy comes with a reputation, don't think you'll change it. Here's a great example: There was this guy in town I had known about for years. I heard his name mentioned by several of my friends, but we had never met. He had an air of intrigue surrounding him, and it drove me crazy. I finally met him at a party. I immediately fell for him because I knew he was a bad boy, and he was super-hot. But evidently I didn't make an impression because the meeting was as far as anything went. We ran into each other here and there over the next year, but he never paid much attention to me. Finally, we ended up on a bike crawl together. Bike crawl + tequila = me sucking face with this guy outside a bar. Everyone had told me he had slept his way through town—hell, even he told me he'd slept his way through town. Did I let that stop me? No. The sex was amazing, we had a ton of fun together, and we got along great because neither one of us cared. No worries, right? Wrong. As soon as I saw his pictures posted all over Facebook with a different girl every night, it was more than a tingle of jealousy I felt. As much as I hate to admit, it does sting a little when you realize you're not the only one on the playing field. This is a grown up game, and you'd better be ready to take some hits from time to time.

Rules about boys who just moved up from the minors. Proceed with extreme caution...that's the only rule. For those of you who seem to either attract or prefer guys much younger than you are, listen up. No doubt, dating younger men is a blast and makes you feel amazing. But, boy toys can turn into big heartbreaks if you're not careful. They will wine and dine you, dote on you, sext you all day, spoil you, tell you how beautiful you are, and tell you how amazing your body is. They'll talk about the future with you, talk about taking this trip and that trip, tell you how much they love having a girl around they can actually talk to, how much they love your uninhibited nature, and how much they love your success. All they want to do is impress you, have lots of fun, please you in bed, and make you happy. Sounds perfect, doesn't it? It is perfect...for a few months. So enjoy it while it lasts, but know it likely won't last long.

Be willing to cut players for the sake of the game. Ever had the 180-day One-Night-Stand? Whether it's the boy next door, the groomsman at the wedding, the cabana boy, the bartender, your best friend's brother, or whatever, recognize it for what it is, and don't let it go too far. As my friend Dar says…I know he's cute, and you want to keep him, but no!

Aim for the triple play. Be fun, flirty, and flexible. Casual dating is all about having an I-am-okay-with-whatever attitude. Keep conversations light, stay away from drama, have fun, and be up for anything.

Don't assume the outcome of any game. Don't assume he is going to call, not call, show up, not show up, want a relationship, not want one, or call after you've had sex. Don't assume you have plans with him this weekend, that he wants to spend the holidays with you, that he'll remember your birthday, etc. Don't even assume he's single. In casual relationships, there are no assumptions and no expectations. No exceptions.

The less you care about winning, the better you will play. Casual relationships are all about power and generally, the one who cares the least has the most power. It's very easy to lose or give away your power when you get caught up in the game. But you need to start with the power and keep it. When you forget about just having fun and start putting expectations on the relationship (and you will know when you have), it's time to call the game and get the hell out of dodge.

Keep the home court advantage—it's always better to have the last at bat. Never be the first one to call. If he is that interested in you, he will call. If he didn't ask for your number, don't volunteer it. If he wants to find you, he will.

If he calls, you call. If he texts, you text. If he sends you a Facebook message, send him one back. If he blows you off, blow him off. If you see him out with another woman, make sure you have another date with someone else the next night. This is not about tricking the other person. These are simply the rules of casual dating. Don't initiate action—just respond to his.

If you've already made contact and are in the middle of an exchange (i.e. he texts you, you text him back, and now he hasn't texted you back), is it okay for you to make contact twice and text him again? No. Absolutely not. It's his turn in the batter's box. If he doesn't step up, sub someone else from the bench. Same goes for phone calls and Facebook messages.

> **Bonus tip:** Whenever I'm dating a guy
> and I'm waiting on him to reach out, I can

never sleep. Can you? Put your cell phone on silent, and then put it outside your door. You won't die I promise. If the phone is in the room with you, you'll be checking it every five minutes. Kate used to come home and crack up when she saw my cell phone outside my bedroom door. But guess what? His call never went straight to voice mail and likely left him wondering where I was... while I got a good night of sleep!

If for some reason you ignore these communication tips, that's fine, but be prepared for the worst. If you want to call, then call. But don't drown yourself in a bottle of vodka when he doesn't answer or doesn't respond to your text, e-mail, or Facebook message. It's casual, remember?

Develop your natural instincts for the game... then trust them. This one takes skill and practice but once mastered it can help you keep things in perspective. All too often, we see red flags covering the sky, but we ignore them because the guy is really cute, or really smart, or really rich, or really good in bed, or really whatever. I'm not telling you to snoop, but I am telling you to look around. Not too much, but keep an eye on things and trust your instincts.

If you think something is wrong, it is. (The tube of women's deodorant that used to be in the back of his bathroom cabinet didn't magically move itself to the front. I'm just sayin'.) Better to have a little fun with the guy and get out quickly than to suffer a heartbreak in a few months.

Beware of world-series emotions when you haven't even made the playoffs. You know the feeling I'm talking about. It's the feeling of flying, crying, laughing, dancing, and throwing up all at the same time. When you're casually dating, this feeling is very dangerous because you can't tell if it's fear, anxiety, happiness, lust, obsession, love, or just heartburn from the leftover cold pizza you ate for breakfast. Realize it's more than likely not love; enjoy the feeling, but don't take it seriously. And, monitor it closely.

Be prepared for rainouts. Go on heightened alert when you're headed for bad weather. There are many times in casual dating when the potential for stormy weather—and maybe the need to delay the game—is high, such as right after the first time you have sex, right after you've shared an intimate moment, and the second you realize you have feelings for the guy. I generally refer to these as Danger Zones. A Danger Zone is a point in the relationship when, if the stars are aligned, you will accidentally fall really hard for a guy. It happens very quickly and sometimes out of nowhere. It's very important for you to notice when this happens and to stop it from going any further. Chances are you're not really into this guy, but emotional circumstances have led you to this point. Notice earlier I said you realize you have feelings for the guy? Generally this is not the case. Generally you just think you have feelings for the guy, but when you break it down, the feelings aren't real. It's important to use extra caution when any of these potential emotional storms are brewing. I can recall several times throughout my life when I've literally said "Oh, Shit" to myself the very second I realized I had fallen for a guy. Those moments are imbedded in my brain, and all of them could have been avoided.

A particularly risky Danger Zone is right after a break up. Be extra careful. Your feelings after a break up are unstable at best. Pay attention to them, but do your best not to act on them. Don't get me wrong— you don't need to be afraid to date, but keep your head straight. Remember you're dating, not looking for "the one."

Eject players when necessary. R.E.S.P.E.C.T. That's what I'm talking about. Just because you're casually dating doesn't mean you allow yourself to be disrespected. Ever. The minute a guy ditches you, stands you up, makes you feel bad, talks down to you, embarrasses you, or ignores you when you're supposed to be hanging out, tell him to f off, and don't look back. Never give respect to a guy who doesn't respect you. Ever.

Never let them see you sweat. This is critical. Before you make a complete ass out of yourself, walk away from any situation where you might be tempted to cry, yell, profess your love, throw a temper tantrum, or worse, throw a set of keys. You are casually dating for fun. You have choice, and you have the power to control yourself and the situation. Call your best friend, and have her talk you off the ledge. If she doesn't answer, keep going down the list until someone does. If you can't get ahold of anyone, go to the gym or do a work-out at home immediately. The endorphins released during exercise will elevate your mood and help you see things clearly.

A forfeit's better than a loss. Don't take it personally when a guy blows you off because you won't have sex with him. Take it as a compliment he had enough guts to blow you off, rather than lead you on to get what he wanted. I've got a great story that goes along with this tip in the Interpreting Guy Behavior chapter.

Use your timeouts. As you're out there casually dating, you'll start to notice your own patterns of behavior. But also know when you're crying on your BFF's shoulder for the tenth time over some guy you knew was not right for you, it's no longer a pattern. It's a problem. It may be time to take a timeout.

There are many times when a little break can be helpful. For example, the bench is empty, and it's taking a little too much effort to find new players. Or, you find yourself too focused on one guy. Or, you've lost sight of yourself and are not taking good care of yourself physically and emotionally. Maybe you're doubting yourself and have lost your edge. Or maybe you've lost touch with your friends. You'll know when you need a timeout…your body will tell you. Take a few weeks to regroup, reenergize, and refocus. You'll be back on the field in no time with more confidence than ever. It says a lot about a woman who can take a timeout for herself, who doesn't always have to be in the center of everything. I take timeouts several times a year, and it always feels good. I usually do a 30-day cleanse, I finish projects around the house, I work out every day, I finally read all the books I've downloaded, etc. Of course, like my friend Lisa says, you might initially suffer from FOMO (fear of missing out). But once you realize how powerful it makes you feel, you'll be just fine.

Drugs only lead to suspensions. If you think you can control your emotions and actions when you're on drugs, think again, especially if you're the least bit attracted to a guy. Partying will only intensify those feelings and make you susceptible to falling too fast for the wrong person. I know this is a downer, but it's critical!

Always have necessary game equipment. This is otherwise affectionately known in my circle as "The Mike Bag." Casual daters are always ready for the next adventure. You should keep the following in your car at all times: workout clothes and tennis shoes (don't forget the socks), a sundress or something you can throw on that won't wrinkle, an extra pair of flip flops or casual shoes to go with it, makeup remover, contact solution, toothpaste, toothbrush, deodorant, travel makeup that just stays in the car, a swimsuit, and, of course, a change of underwear. You need to be ready to go wherever, whenever, and if the date is going great, you don't want to have to interrupt it to go home and change.

By the same token, you want to make sure you have everything you need actually on you when you go out at night. My friends make fun of me, but I keep the following in my handbag at all times: travel size toothpaste, a wisk toothbrush, a contact solution holder with solution already in it, Goody headache powders, Alka Seltzer, and Xanax. You never know where you might end up taking a cab to at the end of the night, and you need to get your hangover under control so you can go straight to breakfast with all your friends the next day.

Some of the best commentators are playing a different game. It sounds cliché, but always have a gay boyfriend on speed dial. Your gay friends will often give you something your girlfriends sometimes can't or won't give you: the truth. If you've got a question and you want an honest answer...you know who to call. Their advice might not always be what you want to hear, but it will always be exactly what you need to hear.

It's not whether you win or lose but how you play the game. As you gain experience casually dating, you'll be able to immediately spot a relationship that won't last. This will be a great day! These have been the best casual relationships of my life. I knew they were going to hurt like hell when they were over, BUT I never lost sight of the fact that they would, one day, be over. So, I went for it, put 100 percent into having fun, and walked away knowing myself and understanding men a lot better.

Know when a game isn't going to last the full nine innings. Wondering how to spot a relationship that won't last? Here are some general examples for you:

It's 1 a.m. on Saturday night, and you just met a guy during last call at the club. This type of relationship will generally last 24-48 hours tops, regardless of how mind blowing the night turns out to be.

You meet a guy who lives in another city, or you meet one while you're on vacation. This type of relationship can actually last awhile if you're willing to put forth the effort, but more often than not, he won't want to put forth shit.

You've met a guy who has a reputation. This type of relationship will generally be super fun, super exciting, and super short.

Some other relationships scenarios to look out for that are general signs it won't last: he's 10+ years younger than you, he talks about his ex, he's constantly trying to get you to step out of your comfort zone sexually, he lives like a teenager, he only reaches out to you late night, he gets too serious too fast and conveys his "feelings" for you within a couple of days or weeks, he cancels plans with you at the last minute, etc. This should give you enough to go on for now!

Never talk about past games or seasons. This includes what went on that summer in Newport Beach, the girl crush you had in college, spring break in Vegas, the threesome you had during Mardi Gras, whatever. It's best not to reveal these types of secrets whether you're casually dating or in a serious relationship. It will ALWAYS come back to bite you in the ass.

Turn that last pitch into a home run. If there's one other thing you need to master besides building a bench, it's making every relationship end with a home run. I always try my best to end things on a high note. It might take me a minute to get over the initial sting of the last pitched strike, but eventually I seize the moment and knock the final pitch out of the park. Maybe it's one last roll in the hay (on your terms), maybe it's a casual happy hour where the two of you chat about who you're seeing, maybe it's a quick wink and smile at him over your shoulder at the club (and that's it). Whatever the final act is, it's an action that communicates, "I enjoyed our time together, and I hope we can be friends." It's a great day when you can successfully remove a guy from the bench without being a drama queen. Cool Chick 101 right there.

Remember the *Reputable Guy*? Our story actually has a great ending. Oh I obsessed over him for a little while, but once I got over it I was able to appreciate what a dynamic, fun guy he was. That's what attracted me to him in the first place. When we see each other now, we joke around about our time together, and I give him a hard time constantly because I know him so well. We're actually really great friends. We run in the same circles, so it was extra important to end things on a high note. I am very proud to say I am friendly with every guy I have ever spent time with.

Learn from every practice, game, and season. Look at every relationship as an opportunity: An opportunity to learn something new about yourself or about men. An opportunity to meet new people, explore new places, and step out of your comfort zone. An opportunity to learn new tricks or to finally speak up and ask for what you want in bed. An opportunity to give in fully to life with reckless abandon—no fear and no regrets.

Stages of the Game:
Three Dating Scenarios

Before we get further into the anatomy of a casual relationship, I thought I'd share with you three common relationship scenarios. In each one I'll take you through what would generally happen from the beginning to the end of each relationship. At the end of this book, we will revisit these stories and rewrite our perfect endings!

Week 1

Scenario 1: You met a cute guy and exchanged numbers, he called you two days later to set up a date, and now you're super excited but a little apprehensive because he isn't exactly what you're looking for.

Scenario 2: You met the perfect guy and exchanged numbers, he called to ask you out for Saturday night. Now you're beyond super excited and already thinking about baby names.

Scenario 3: You met a super-hot guy (total bad boy, of course) while out with your friends, got drunk, and went home with him. You felt like shit because you knew there was a strong possibility you may not hear from him again, but then three days later he texts you and wants to get together. Yay! Whew.

Weeks 2 – 4

Scenario 1: You've been on a couple of dates, but there's no spark. You decide to keep him around because he's the perfect guy for certain occasions— you know, the occasions when you need a date who won't embarrass you? Yeah, this guy's perfect for that. Let's call him Steady Eddie.

Scenario 2: You've gone out once with Mr. Perfect, and you're glad you did because as you suspected…he's perfect! He's charming, funny, successful, gorgeous— and a gentleman. He didn't even try to kiss you. You can see him being a blast around your friends, and don't even get me started about mom. She'll love him.

Scenario 3: You met up with Bad Boy Bill for happy hour on Friday night and didn't come up for air until Saturday afternoon.

Month 2

Scenario 1: Steady Eddie has proven to be a great running buddy. You've gone hiking, clubbing, out to the movies, and out to dinner a few times, and still you've never been at a loss for conversation or laughs. And bonus, it turns out he likes Indian food and Indy films as much as you do. He was a great date for your cousin's wedding (which ended with the two of you in bed together—not bad, actually). This is turning out to be a great guy!

Scenario 2: It's been a whirlwind romance with Mr. Perfect. Nice dinners and weekend trips, and he gives you little gifts all the time to show how much he's thinking about you. He's responsive, the sex is amazing, you have long talks about your goals and dreams…you're thinking about asking him to go home with you for the holidays because you can't wait for your family to meet him. He's still so perfect!

Scenario 3: You're still having a great time with Bad Boy Bill…whenever he texts you that is, which is usually Saturday at 3 a.m. You don't read into it too much because you know it's just for "fun," and the sex is out of this world. He's so hot.

Month 3

Scenario 1: Steady Eddie has turned into steady for sure—you guys are hanging out a lot. You know he's seeing other girls, and he knows you're seeing other guys, which is not a problem until one night you're lying there after you've had sex (which has gotten much better by the way), and suddenly it hits you: you really like this guy. Maybe you overlooked how great he is because he didn't fit your picture of perfection. Maybe it's time to give him a real chance. He might be more than a backup guy after all!

Scenario 2: Mr. Perfect is MIA. It's been two weeks since you've seen him. You've exchanged texts and voice mails, but you can't seem to get your schedules together. The holidays are coming up, and you really want to talk to him about plans.

Scenario 3: You run into Bad Boy Bill one night at the club, and he gives you a wink over the shoulder of the hot blonde he's got his arm around. You see him later that night at another club, and he's alone. You guys chat it up for a while, have a hot make-out session in the corner, then go off with your respective friends. You're certain he'll text you later. The club closes and no text...so you text him. No response, so you text again 30 minutes later. Still no response, so you text one more time, "Heading home, babe. Hit me up if you're coming over!" No response.

Months 4 – 5

Scenario 1: Believe what you will about guys, but one thing I know: they have expert radar for true feelings. Steady Eddie can sense your newfound feelings for him, and now he's started to pull away. You're not getting together as often, he's not as "available" as he once was, he's cancelled plans with you a few times, and now you're analyzing every, single, small detail of the last three months to try and figure out what you did wrong.

Scenario 2: You spent two weeks in bed crying over Mr. Perfect, who has disappeared. You can't understand what happened. Everything seemed so… perfect. The family is asking if he's still coming for the holidays, and you don't know what to tell them. You can't tell them the truth: Mr. Perfect seduced you, then stopped calling when he got bored. Now you're alone and pissed at yourself for blowing off all the other guys for this one.

Scenario 3: Bad Boy Bill sends you a random text every now and then, but never follows through on meeting up. You know he's only doing it to make sure you're still on the hook. Still, you don't have enough strength to tell him to f off, even though you know he has no intention of reeling you in. There's just something about him you can't let go of. He's so hot.

Month 6:

Scenario 1: A strange car is parked outside Steady Eddie's house. You think he's seeing someone else. Not that you drive by often…just after you've been drinking…which happens to be a lot lately. How did you let this happen? You didn't even really like him to begin with. He was just a backup! Now look at you: a crazy, drive-by bitch. No wonder he avoids you like the plague and never responds to your texts.

Scenario 2: Mr. Perfect called the other day to see if you were free for dinner. Luckily, you already had another date lined up for that night so it was easy to say, "Sorry, I've got other plans." You were sure he'd ask you out for a different night, but he didn't. When he said goodbye, you knew that was the last time you'd hear from him. It feels like he just twisted a knife deep inside your gut.

Scenario 3: The soft flame of desire still burns for Bad Boy Bill, and you have a feeling it will linger for a while. You read somewhere *Bad boys are bad for a reason… because they're bad.* Even though you now know firsthand how true this is, you still can't resist them!

The Master

5

The Master

This next story is a great introduction to the next Chapter, *Absolute Bliss*. It illustrates how easy it is to let the butterflies take control of your emotions quickly after you meet a guy you really like. It also illustrates how easy it is to ignore certain signs a relationship isn't meant to last. You see, when a woman meets a guy she really likes, and she's on a mission to find a boyfriend, she will typically overlook certain things because she really wants to be in a relationship. There's nothing wrong with wanting to be in a relationship, but again, that's not what we're talking about here. We're talking about meeting a guy, having fun, taking the pressure off, and letting the relationship go where it goes. If things naturally move into something more serious then great. But if things don't, be strong enough to move on.

Back in my husband hunting days, I had just arrived in Phoenix from Atlanta to start a new job. I was staying with my parents because I wasn't actually moving for another few months. I had been there about two weeks when I met the man I now affectionately refer to as The Master.

We met in line at Togo's, which was a popular lunch place for professionals across the street from my office. He had on a beautiful suit and nice shoes (another clincher for me), was totally charming, immediately engaged me in conversation, complimented me on my outfit, asked if I was new in town (this should have been my first clue), and asked me about my job. During our conversation we discovered we were in a similar line of work. Then we got our lunch and went our separate ways. I wasn't back in the office five minutes when my phone rang. It was him. Resourceful—I hadn't given him my number. I was quite impressed to say the least, and he asked me out for lunch the next day.

When he showed up the next day to pick me up for lunch, he had a present—a carrying case for my cell phone. It was super thoughtful, and I turned into super smitten. I'd never really gone out with a guy who was so attentive so early on. It was exhilarating. We went on several lunch dates over the next week or so, and he always showed up with a little gift. He didn't try to kiss me until our fourth lunch date. All of his behaviors were playing right into the first-comes-love-then-comes-marriage fantasy I was still hooked on. He seemed to be serious about me…clearly not interested in just hooking up. I thought there was real potential here, and I was really excited about it. Too excited.

Our first big dinner date was at AZ88, a trendy, upscale Phoenix hot spot. Over dinner, we had a long conversation about plans, futures, dreams, etc., and during this conversation, I made it crystal-clear to him I was not interested in a casual relationship. He agreed, and said he was looking for something more substantial, too. It was a perfect evening, and I was giddy because I seriously thought I'd hit the jackpot. He was good-looking, funny, and successful. He had style and was easy to talk to, and I knew my mom would love him. That night, I went home with him. I remember because I had not planned on going home with him, and I didn't have any toiletries with me. So, we stopped at the grocery store, and he picked up everything I needed. I was like, "Wow, this is really happening to me!"

He continued to buy me little gifts, doted on me, and took me out for lunches and dinners, talked about the future, gave me his undivided attention, talked to me about anything and everything for hours on end, and was amazing around my friends. He made me feel so sexy and even liked it when I used my vibrator. I was in heaven for sure. That shit's hard to find.

Naturally, as women do, I started expecting certain things out of our relationship—one month in. For example, I expected him to call and make plans with me before the weekend. I also expected him to let me know what his plans were—daily. I expected him to want to spend his free time with me. All of it. I started asking questions about the suspicions I had about him seeing other women, etc. You know the drill. So what do you think happened next? The relationship lasted all of two months before ending abruptly. I was crushed—again.

But there was a silver lining with this one. Suddenly and finally, I saw a pattern. I could see how I jumped into relationships too fast rather than just dating and seeing what happens. I was always paying attention to the future instead of enjoying the present. I was trying to control the relationship instead of letting it unfold more naturally. And, I could see I was more suffocating than a dry-cleaning bag. Who's going to want to play and have fun with a dry-cleaning bag? Besides a cat? Oh, and did I forget to mention Key-Throwing Crazy Bitch surfaced again? Oh yeah… drive-bys and all. It was not a good situation.

Looking back now, I realize what a gift that was. Not many of us realize we are in a bad pattern of behavior, let alone have it hit us as clear and cold as a chilled Belvedere dirty martini thrown in the face. I could have gone on and on thinking it was always "the guy's fault," that every guy was just a jerk. I could have gotten stuck at, "Why does this keep happening to me? What could possibly be wrong with me? I'm perfect!"

It's easy to get stuck there. Your friends tend to reinforce those beliefs, too. I know they're trying to be helpful with their "What an asshole" responses. But they just help keep you in the same miserable holding pattern, going in circles, never landing, and not enjoying the ride.

Well girls, luckily, I am not your friend. I am here to tell you how it is—how to stop landing on icy runways and start heading to sunny, fun-focused destinations.

Want to know what happened to The Master? We actually stayed friends (and are still friends to this day). We ran into each other all the time socially and otherwise. I caved and had sex with him here and there, thinking it would lead us back together. It didn't. A couple of years ago we ran into each other at a conference, and I told him about the book. You see The Master is my muse, and I wanted him to know. I wanted to thank him for what he'd done for me. I wasn't kidding when I said my pattern hit me across the face. I was in a moving truck with my brother Scott, driving my things across the country from Georgia to Phoenix, when I grabbed a notepad and started jotting down what had happened with The Master. It was amazing how the floodgates opened. It was fun and helpful for Scott to witness this moment, and he actually gave me a few of his own experiences to jot down. But when it was all said and done, there it was on paper…my broken-record life being played over and over again right in front of my eyes.

Would things have turned out differently with The Master if I knew what I know now? Not really. Yes, the relationship would have played out differently, but it would've ended just the same. How do I know that? I named him The Master for a reason. Had I known what I know now, I would have immediately been able to recognize how he played me from the moment we met. How he buttered me up without physical contact. How he knew exactly what to say and when to say it. How he told me exactly what he knew I wanted to hear. And guess what… after spending some time in Phoenix, I met several other girls just like me who had been "masterfully" played by him as well. Oh and this should have been my second clue...his favorite movie was American Psycho. If you haven't seen it, rent it. If any guy tells you he loves this movie...run.

Remember the tip *develop your natural instincts for the game*...and then, most importantly, trust them? It was in The Master's medicine cabinet I saw the mysterious tube of women's deodorant move from the back to the front. I saw this on a Monday after we'd spent the weekend apart from each other. We spent the weekend apart because he was "busy." Gotta give the guy props though...he was good.

6

Absolute Bliss:
The Beginning of a Casual Relationship

The beginning of a casual relationship is fun and exciting. The butterflies in your stomach are alive; and you start having he-could-be-the-one thoughts.

But listen up! Don't be fooled. These feelings do not mean anything. Period. Just enjoy them for what they are and understand from the beginning they will not last. I'm talking three, four months tops.

Also understand those amazing feelings muddle your judgment: I know he smokes, but that's okay. I know he's unemployed right now, but it's temporary. I know I'm old enough to be his mother, but we can make it work. I know he is in the middle of a divorce, but that's cool. I know he's got a reputation, but things will be different with me. I know he's not exactly bench material, but that's okay—I can mold him. You make concessions and ignore your instincts and end up devastated when Prince Charming turns out to be sit-on-the-couch Larry—or Bad-Boy Bill. Remember him? The sooner you throw a net over those butterflies and pay attention, the more likely you'll save yourself a lot of heartache and avoid throwing keys at strangers' windows. Here are some tips to help keep your head clear, while still enjoying that blissful feeling!

Keep it in perspective. Don't get too excited about any casual relationship. You know you're getting carried away when you can hear wedding bells and it's only been four dates.

Don't be an eager beaver. I know your heart nearly stops every time he calls, but every once in a while, even if you don't have plans, pretend you do. It will make him want you that much more. Trust me. Let his calls go to voice mail every now and then. Wait at least three hours before you return his call, etc. Same with text messages and email: don't text or email right back. There will always be another opportunity, so just chill!

Confirm the date. If he doesn't confirm the date, make other plans. There is nothing worse than thinking you have plans with guy #1, and therefore you tell guy #2 you are busy. Then guy #1 flakes out at the last minute. You can't call guy #2 because then he will know he was second up to bat. Guy #3 is out of town. You see my point. Confirm the date at least a day in advance, then again the day of. When casually dating, it's too easy to blow people off. Don't let it happen to you. On the same token, if you did confirm the date, and he's more than 30 minutes late without calling, do something else immediately. Do not, and I repeat, do not wait around for a guy to show up. Screw that. You've got better things to do. You had a backup plan right?

Daddy always said. Have enough money to pay for your own dinner, a cab, a hotel room, or a plane ticket. Let's see...I have been stranded in San Diego, Dallas, Paris, Wyoming, and Chicago, and I wasn't living in any of those cities at the time. You never know when a situation is going to blow up. Have friends or family you can call at all times to help get you out of a jam, too.

Taxi! We touched on this a little already—always have your own transportation, or money for it. Meet him out and leave your car close by, or meet up with some friends to get a ride—whatever. Just don't leave yourself with the possibility of being stranded. It's torture when you're ready to leave, or even worse when you can sense he's ready for you to leave, or when it becomes absolutely necessary to leave because you suddenly realize three of the five guys on your bench are all at the same f'ing club with you! Actually, you may not want to call a taxi in this situation—you should probably call a moving company.

Let chivalry lie. Even if he offers to come pick you up, it's best to meet him out to avoid any uncomfortable goodbyes at the end of the night. Most guys will do or say whatever is necessary to make sure they're invited in after they drop you off. Don't put yourself in the position in the first place early on, unless of course that's what you want—then go for it!

Check, please! In my opinion, you should always offer to pay for your own dinner. When the check comes, just reach for your billfold, and see what happens. This sends a clear signal you are not the girl who's just out for a free meal. Be very gracious when he does pay, and be very gracious when he lets you pay. If he does let you pay, don't let it be a deal-breaker in a casual relationship. There are lots of girls out there who use guys for free meals, free transportation, free lodging, or free whatever they can get their hands on and some guys won't stand for it. Good for them.

No-friend zone. Unless you want all of the fun you're having to blow up in your face, don't friend any guy you are dating casually on any social media site. Or, you can do like I do—I only have pictures of me and my friends on Facebook. I will never post a picture of me with a guy on Facebook, unless for some crazy reason I find myself in a relationship. It's rare for me to even let myself get photographed with a guy…too risky.

By this same token, Facebook is crack cocaine for Crazy Bitch. Nothing brings Crazy Bitch to the scene faster than seeing pictures of guys you're dating with other women, even though you're out there doing the same thing. Now there's a Double Standard in Dating for you. If you think you can handle it, then great, friend away. But when you see a pic of your favorite bencher on Facebook with his arms around another girl, suck it up, do a shot, and don't let it ruin your day.

Gauge your own interest. You don't have to be interested in him just because he is interested in you. I've fallen into this trap many times. I thought if a guy was pursuing me then I must be really lucky and special. Wrong. Well, you *are* special, but not necessarily to him. Chances are he is pursuing a few other women, too. By the same token, if you meet a guy and he's just okay but pursues you, then it's totally up to you if you want to accept the advance. I have ended up in some really great relationships with some amazing men who I thought were just okay in the beginning. Gotta give a guy a chance!

Too close for comfort. Avoid dating your neighbor, anyone you work with, anyone in your apartment building, friends of the family, family members of your friends, etc. If you value your privacy at home, your job, or your family relationships…enough said.

Sleepover! Sleepovers can be lots of fun—until the next morning. It's one of two things in the beginning of a casual relationship: either the sleepover lasts for days, and you think you're in love; or it's awkward as hell the morning after, and you have no idea what to do or if you will ever see this guy again. Either way, it's *no bueno*. If you can, tell him what a great time you had and how wonderful he was, but don't stay the night. If you must, though, I suggest spending no more than one night together at a time. And, if you absolutely can't help yourself, for heaven's sake stay at his house so you can leave when you want to!

My home is my castle. This goes along with sleeping over. Inviting a guy into your home is okay, but just be clear about your intentions. If you want to sleep with him, fine. If you don't, you'd better be prepared to ward off his advances. To most guys, being invited into your home is code for "We are having sex."

Sunday is my day! It's okay to spend Friday OR Saturday night together, but definitely not both nights and definitely not Sunday night. Sunday is for family time, relaxing, day drinking with your friends, lounging around in your skivvies with your hair in a ponytail, gearing up for the week ahead...and of course, watching _True Blood_.

The lion's den. It's hard to avoid introducing a casual relationship to your friends. Just don't introduce him as you would a new puppy (i.e., with "Isn't he cute!" "Isn't he sweet!" or "Isn't he perfect!"). Everyone will get all excited and start telling you how great he is, how perfect you are together, etc. On that same note, absolutely do NOT introduce him to any family member for at least six months. Maybe even a year if you're still together by then. In fact, I wouldn't even tell anyone in your family about any guy on the bench until you are ready to clear it off and focus on just one. The last guy I introduced to my family was my high school prom date, and they are still talking about him! Okay, that's maybe a bit of an exaggeration, but not much of one. You don't know my family.

Wheels up? As much as jetting off to Mexico for the weekend sounds like a blast, I would avoid trips initially. Weekends together will put your emotions on the superhighway, and before you know it, you can't get off. Or worse, you suddenly realize you're on the superhighway by yourself because your travel partner took the nearest exit off. Guys can do casual weekend trips, no problem. It's a little harder for us because we get emotionally tied quickly, especially when we're being sexed up on the beach in Cabo. I'm not saying it can't ever be done, but just be careful and watch your emotions.

The early bird gets the worm. If you're not his 7 p.m. date, don't be his 10 p.m. date, and certainly not his 2 a.m. date. Just because you want to date casually doesn't mean you have to be the casual booty call.

Channel Vivian. Think *Pretty Woman*, and don't kiss on the mouth. This was a great piece of advice and one that truly works. Creating close and sensual moments early on in a relationship can cause you to fall too quickly.

Playing House. Let's say you've been seeing a guy for about a month. You decide to invite him over for a nice dinner that took you all day to prepare. Three bottles of wine and 10 hours later you've talked, "made love," made plans, and basked in the glow of what has just been the most amazing night you've had in a really long time. I hope you enjoyed yourself because I guaran-damn-tee he will pull away from you. I'd venture to say you won't see him again for at least two weeks, if ever. Oh, he may reach out to you, but not as often as he was before, and it will eventually fizzle out faster than you expected. This generalization is the same for any "intimate" moment early on in a casual relationship, like sharing a family crisis or suffering a serious illness with him. Guys just aren't equipped to handle this level of intimacy in a casual relationship. And honestly, they don't really want to. Oh, it feels good to them while it's happening, but the morning after, they'll have an emotional hangover for sure and will start looking for a way out. Sure, it's fun to play house when you're casually dating, but only for a minute, and don't expect it to be a normal occurrence. Romantic evenings at home can be really nice and comforting, as long as you know it's not the road to Coupleville.

Party girl—don't be one. I am all about having fun, but this is where I get in trouble every single time. It's so easy to get caught up in all the fun you're having, the laughing, dancing, and clubbing all night, but limit use of drugs and alcohol for the first five dates—at least—so you can decide how you want the relationship to go. Drugs and alcohol intensify feelings, or worse, create feelings that aren't real. Keeping the situation under control helps you control your uncontrollable self.

Keep it to yourself. Casually dating means just that. It's casual, it's fun, and it's temporary. There is no need to reveal anything about yourself, like your hopes of having children, your dream to be America's next Top Chef, your family history, your past experiences, your fear of getting hurt. These conversations should be reserved for serious relationships. Discussing them now could compromise what you are out to accomplish: Having fun! Some guys out there will try to coerce this information out of you. Beware of this guy. He is more than likely not really interested in getting to know you, but more interested in having the information to control you or navigate his way into your pants. No man out there wants to know everything about you. Most men honestly couldn't care less about your past or current dramas—especially men casually dating. They don't want to know how your last relationship ended. They don't want to know how long it's been since you've had a real date. They don't want to know about your family drama. It's best if you act a little mysterious all the time, as if you're hiding something juicy on purpose. It will create attraction and intrigue. Let them think you have a secret with a seductive wink and a smile.

See you next year! Spending holidays together and buying gifts for each other is off limits. It's rather hard and can get really expensive when you're dating five guys after all. It's best to just enjoy the time with your family. Sure, it's okay to send a "Happy Thanksgiving" text, but no more than that. And don't read into it if he sends a text to you. It's just a text. Holidays are for loved ones and friends.

Ready yet? Getting ready at his place leads to unnecessary anxiety. You are unconsciously looking around, looking for clues, looking for girl evidence, etc. Why put yourself through that kind of torture?

Promises, promises. In the blissful beginning of a relationship, both of you are excited. Yes, he's excited, too. It's new, it's fresh, it's fun, it's unpredictable, and it's a bunch of B.S. You're putting on a show for him, and he's promising the world to you. He'll promise to do this and that with you. He'll talk about taking you to this restaurant and that club. He'll talk about booking this and that trip. He'll talk about buying you this thing or that thing. Whatever promises are made during this time will more than likely never come to pass. So just go along with it, and promise to do a bunch of shit for him, too.

Runaway train. When you're casually dating, it is so easy to let your thoughts run away with you. Just because he hasn't responded to your text from yesterday, you've decided this guy's a complete asshole and think, "What the hell is he doing that he can't respond back to my text?" You've already decided he's with someone else, he's lost interest in you, you did something wrong. You've already called all your girlfriends to tell them what an asshole he is, and you've rehearsed the whole conversation in your mind you plan to have with him when he does text back, which includes both "How dare you" and "Go f**k yourself." Take a breath. A deep one. Step back, hide your phone, and go take a run or something or something. He will text you back eventually, and when he does, don't make a big deal out of it. He's not an asshole. This is supposed to be casual... remember?

Slow your roll. When I first started casually dating, I had to learn how to hold back on my emotions. It was really easy for me to fall for a guy quickly, especially after we'd had sex. Virtually every guy I met could potentially be "the one" because all had great qualities, were a lot of fun, and treated me well. I had to reel myself in a bunch, and it took me a while to get the hang of it. I would suggest observing yourself in various relationships to see when you start to fall. If you can see the pattern, then you can break it.

Friends with benefits. The friends-with-benefits arrangement can be amazing as long as both of you can keep your emotions out of it. Otherwise, it becomes a sure-fire way to lose a friend and gain a heartache.

Don't be that friend. Don't you just hate the friend who blows everyone off and cancels plans after she meets someone? I understand wanting to spend time with a new guy, but ditching your friends at the last minute is lame. If you have plans with your friends, keep them. If you have plans in general, keep them. Don't offer to go out of your way or make serious compromises early on for a guy, and certainly don't switch up your schedule to see a guy because it works better for him.

Side Note: If you're "that friend" and everyone knows it, try this strategy: If you sort of have plans with a guy but the girls are wanting you to meet up with them for happy hour, set the situation up so you have an out if you need it. Example: "I'll more than likely meet you guys for happy hour, but I'm not 100 percent sure. I'll text you if I can make it." This way you're open to meet up with the guy but have a backup plan if he doesn't come through. Everyone's happy, and no one feels slighted.

The Breakthrough

The Breakthrough

I had just decided to move to L.A., and of course, two weeks before I was ready to hit the road, I met the man of my dreams, aka The Breakthrough. I called my girlfriend Stacey that night on the way home and said, "I think God is playing a cosmic joke on me because I just met the perfect guy right here in Scottsdale!" The Breakthrough was from the Middle East and was literally tall, dark, and handsome. He radiated style, culture, and confidence. Not only did he challenge me intellectually, but he was also very affectionate and passionate. He was a true gentleman. And, he let me know right off the bat he could see right through me, which immediately created a feeling of comfort and safety for me. His sex appeal was off the charts, and despite the fact I was moving, I absolutely could not help myself.

From the get-go, I knew this relationship would be amazing—and I also knew it wouldn't last long. A brand-new, extremely passionate, soon-to-be long-distance relationship would never make it. I think that was probably part of the appeal to both of us: me leaving.

For the first time in my life, I made the adult woman choice to enter into a casual relationship I knew would not last. I distinctly remember saying out loud to myself, "This is going to hurt like hell when it's over." But I jumped in and enjoyed it while it lasted, which ended up being about a year. If you boil it down to actual time spent together however, the actual life span of the relationship was (you guessed it) about three months.

We did the back and forth thing every few months, and every time we saw each other it was a Fourth of July fireworks show. We took trips together, shared intimate moments, and talked about our lives. Since I had nothing to lose, I threw myself in 100 percent just to see what would happen. I didn't hold back one bit. If I felt it, I said it. If I wanted to see him, I drove to Phoenix. If I wanted to talk to him, I called. I let go in bed and really enjoyed myself without wondering where the relationship was going. I enjoyed every minute as it if were our last, and I didn't try to make the relationship into something it wasn't. And guess what? I didn't die when it ended.

From this moment on, I was able to see dating from an entirely different perspective. I know you've heard the old adage, "Better to have loved and lost than never to have loved at all." This is absolutely true in casual dating. I know this may sound crazy, but start with the end in mind. If you do, when the end comes, it won't hurt nearly as bad. You'll be able to appreciate what you just experienced and have no hard feelings when it's time to let go.

8

Bliss Meets Reality:
The Middle of a Casual Relationship

The middle of a casual relationship is still pretty awesome, but it's also pretty dangerous. You've been seeing each other for several weeks now and spending regular time together. The sex is amazing, and you find yourself fantasizing about him when you're not together. You can start to predict his behavior. He usually texts you on Friday afternoon to see what you're up to over the weekend, and you usually go out either Friday or Saturday night (or both sometimes). If you're out with your respective friends, you always hook up at the end of the night. He responds immediately to your texts for the most part. And, you've broken the rule and spent more than one night together. In other words, you're starting to get a little comfortable and starting to expect certain behaviors, like that text on Friday afternoon. Remember when I said there are no expectations in casual dating, no exceptions? Well, now is when you'll truly be put to the test.

For example...

It's Friday at 5 p.m., and you haven't heard from him. Then you see his posts on Facebook. He's out with his friends, but he didn't tell you he had plans. You text him the next day, and he doesn't respond until much later in the day, if at all. It's Sunday now, and you're wondering if you're going to see him this weekend. You're a little hurt, but you try to remind yourself you're just casually dating. You make plans with friends Sunday afternoon, but you spend the whole time talking about him. You finally connect on Tuesday and decide to meet for dinner. Dinner is awesome. You go back to your place and have mind-blowing, I-miss-you sex. You think he's spending the night as usual, but he says he needs to get up early for work and leaves. You feel a little weird, but the sex was so good everything must be okay.

So this is where we are...bliss meeting reality. You're still really excited about this guy, and he seems to be into you. BUT, the usual patterns of behavior are starting to be broken. You communicate less and less, and you're in a constant state of confusion. You're not sure if you feel happy because you're still having a great time or scared because you sense something has changed. There's no getting around it: these feelings suck. And if you're not careful, they can quickly turn something that's going just fine into something going very wrong—key-throwing, crazy wrong.

But, hide your keys, and don't panic. I can help. These feelings are normal and tolerable when you know how to handle them. Following are tips to help you still have fun while keeping Crazy Bitch at bay.

Do it yourself. Don't ask him to help you with anything—moving, buying a car, buying a house, fixing the toilet, picking out furniture, picking out lingerie, anything. This will only make you want him around more and/or might lead him to believe you want him around more and/or might make him want to be around more when, really, you don't actually want him around more, and he actually doesn't want to help you.

No explanations necessary. You don't need to explain how you feel, why you're doing something a certain way, why you don't call back immediately, why you aren't married, why you have to go home, why you can't spend more than two nights in a row. It is what it is. Explain it to your friends, not him. He certainly isn't going to explain himself to you—nor should he.

Don't be a slave to your phone. If you find yourself sitting around waiting on his call, turn your phone off, and go do something. Yes, you can survive for a few hours without a phone. It's actually quite nice. If it's nighttime, turn your phone off, and go to bed. Like I said earlier, you might even want to put it outside your bedroom door so you aren't tempted to check it every five minutes. And don't give yourself the excuse of "I have to keep my phone on in case of an emergency." There are all kinds of phone settings now that let you have the phone on silent, while designated calls from important people will still ring through. And just so we're clear...no guy on the bench should be on the "important people" list.

Harness holiday greetings. We chatted about this a little already. If you're dating during the holidays, don't call him on the holiday. If he calls you, let it go to voice mail, and call him a couple of days later. If he texts you, then text back, but don't be the one to send the initial "Merry Christmas" text. And like I said earlier, if he texts you or calls you on a holiday, don't read into it. Maybe he's just a nice person and wants to wish you a Happy Thanksgiving. Chances are he probably sent that text to several other people too.

No vacation communication. This is the same as holiday greetings. It's best not to call him or communicate while you are on vacation with your friends or family. Checking in with someone you're dating every few hours, or even every day, while you're on vacation is the opposite of casual.

Take some advice from Grandma—don't call boys. This is an old school way of thinking, but it still applies. As a rule, don't call boys; let them call you. If a guy wants to call you, he will. If he wants to talk to you, he will call. If he wants to see you, he will set up a date. Get my drift? If he doesn't call, oh well. You have five other guys on the bench, and I bet one of them is calling!

Avoid TMI. Don't volunteer information about yourself. If he doesn't ask, he isn't interested. Besides, revealing too much about yourself can be risky. One, he could, and very well might, use it against you. Two, once the relationship is over, you'll wish you hadn't divulged your secrets to someone so insignificant.

Forget the whole truth and nothing but.... You're not in court. You don't have to tell the whole story. Remember we chatted about being mysterious and pretending you have a secret? All pretending aside, some things should be kept a secret—forever. You're just casually dating. What you do—or did—with your own time is none of his business.

Keep the upper hand. It's so easy to lose your confidence in the middle of a relationship because things start to get complicated and you're not sure what to do next. You think things are going well, but he's starting to act a little differently. You think things are still fun, but he's not responding to you quite as quickly. You assumed you would see him over the weekend, but it's Monday now and all you did was exchange random text messages. You want to start putting expectations on the relationship, but you know you shouldn't. In order to keep the upper hand you need to be able to recognize what stage of the relationship you're in, and act accordingly. Since we are in the middle, I would suggest things like turning your phone off from time to time when you know he is going to call, not responding to his text messages right away, or blowing him off to hang with your girlfriends. When he asks for an explanation? No explanation necessary! Listen, some of you may be thinking this tip is really shitty behavior, but guess what…guys are doing this to us all the time. These are unfortunately the rules of casual dating and you need to adapt. And to be honest, guys like it when you have the upper hand. It's when you lose the upper hand and in turn lose your confidence, that they lose interest.

Live your life! While you are casually dating, make sure you have many other activities going on like yoga, cooking classes, hang gliding, or whatever keeps you happy. Keep a regular workout schedule, get enough sleep, eat well, and fill up your social calendar with a variety of things to keep yourself from getting into a rut. Going out to the same bars every weekend and seeing the same guys will not satisfy your needs. Plan events with friends and family—and don't change those plans for him. You're a strong, confident, single woman. Now act like one!

If the real is too far from the representative, move on. You generally date someone's "representative" for the first few months. The guy is (or should be) on his best behavior. While no one can be perfectly well-behaved all the time, if you witness major character changes as the relationship continues, immediately kick him off the team and add someone new to the bench.

Allow for alone time. If you've had a bad day, if you don't feel well, if you are feeling melancholy in any way, shape, or form, stay home, or do something with the girls. Guys want girls who are fun. Always be fun to go out with. If you are not in the mood to be fun, don't go.

Wait it out. Don't call him every day, or text every day, or whatever. If you don't hear from him, wait a week, then call or text him—but only if you're in the right frame of mind. If you're sitting around stewing about the fact that he hasn't reached out, then you just need to chill until that feeling goes away. Reaching out while you're feeling irritated will not end well. Trust me, he can sense the desperation in your communication. Once you're in the right frame of mind, reach out to him and see what happens.

Remember what they say about A-S-S-U-M-E. Making assumptions about plans can backfire on both of you, so it's best not to assume you have plans until you confirm. If you want to give a guy a chance, then set him up for success by telling him up front it's important to you for him to confirm plans two days in advance. If after a month he's still ignoring this request—goodbye!

Call BS. In today's age of technology, if a guy is more than 30 minutes late meeting you without any communication at all, it's bullshit. I give you permission to leave—then don't take his calls for at least three days.

Pack it up! Don't leave anything at his place, even if for some reason you're breaking the aforementioned rule about staying two nights in a row. Even if you're planning to come back in a few days. Getting all comfortable in a guy's place is a Danger Zone. Period.

Give a little, but not a lot. It's okay to put some effort into casual relationships; it's even fun and very satisfying sometimes. However, if you aren't getting the same or more in return, then what's the point? You are casually dating for you. Don't give more than you get.

Stay in the honeymoon stage. The fun thing about casually dating is staying in the honeymoon stage for, well, the entire term of the relationship! In fact, that's when you know it's time to get out—when the honeymoon is over.

Save workouts for the gym. If you are working on your relationship more than you are working out at the gym, the honeymoon is definitely over. Time to move on.

Check yourself. You're not in a serious relationship with this guy, so don't treat him like you would someone you're in love with. It's only been a month. Get a grip.

Hey! That's my line! Everyone uses lines (I got tied up with a client, my cell phone died, my cell service sucks, I had no reception, I have a friend in trouble, I fell asleep, my dog is sick), but it pisses me off when a guy uses one of my lines on me. I always play along though as if I have no clue, just to see where it goes. Whatever the line is, just realize it's a line and also probably a preamble to what's next: the end.

Own it. You know who you are, so be that powerful woman who doesn't have to prove herself. You're single, you love being single, you're into your career, you have a full and happy life, and you're having a blast dating a bunch of guys. Don't apologize for this, and don't let anyone make you feel bad for being this way.

The Digression

9

The Digression

Remember the tip *Too Close for Comfort*? Well here's the story behind that one. I was well into writing this book and felt pretty confident in my casual dating ability. That is until The Digression gave me a reality check.

I had been living in L.A. for a while but was starting to think about moving back to Phoenix because I really missed my life there and was finished having my fun in L.A.. I started looking for a new job, but at this point had not secured anything. Then came along… The Digression. I met him at a happy hour event, and I liked him immediately. But, he had a girlfriend. I was bummed but went about my daily life not really thinking of him much.

A few weeks later he called. At first I was surprised, but then I was excited because I suddenly realized he had felt something for me, too! He had gone out of his way to get my number from a mutual friend of ours, so I knew he must really be interested in me. I asked about his girlfriend, and he said they had broken up…sweet!

We made a lunch date, which turned into a dinner date, which turned into drinks, which turned into us going back to my place. Despite a serious attraction, believe it or not, we didn't fool around, just talked and had a great time. He was fun and funny, and we had deep philosophical conversations that night.

At this point on the timeline of my casual dating transformation, I was still not quite comfortable with the whole idea of casual sex. I knew myself well enough to know if I slept with this guy, I'd fall hard for him. If it was going to happen, I needed to know what we had was more than casual. I thought I was being super careful by holding out until I knew for sure he and his ex were truly over. I believed him when he said they were through, though it had only been a month since they broke up. From what he told me though, the relationship had been rocky for a while, and that made me feel more comfortable. He and I were spending more and more time together, sharing more and more intimacy, until one day I finally cracked and had to have sex with him.

Although we never officially established exclusivity, we spent most of our weekends together, introduced each other to friends, and did regular boyfriend/ girlfriend stuff. He introduced me to his brother, for example, and I took him to a work function, something I never do while casually dating. In my mind all of this meant we were "together."

So, here's one tiny detail I've left out thus far: We lived in the same apartment community. Remember what I said about not dating a neighbor, co-worker, friend of the family, etc.? I had been breaking my rules left and right, but this one, as you'll see, turned out to be the most critical.

The Digression and I lived on separate floors, which had helped keep at least a little healthy distance between us. But then my mom and dad came to visit and stayed in one of the corporate apartments in my community. And, you guessed it—their apartment happened to be on the same floor as his. To get my parents to their parking spot, I had to drive by his parking spot. On the day my parents arrived I ushered them to their parking spot and on the way casually looked over to where his car was normally parked. Much to my surprise, his space had somebody else's car in it. I was a little taken aback but didn't make a big deal out of it.

For the rest of the weekend, I didn't see the strange car parked in his spot again. But when we got together next, I asked him who's car it was. He was honest and said his ex-girlfriend's. I was like…okay…and asked why her car was parked there. He told me she had been stranded and needed help, so she called him. Again, I was like…okay…and asked why she called him and not someone else. He said she didn't have much support in the area, he felt bad for her, and he helped her out. I was like….okay….no biggie, a one-time deal. I can handle that. I didn't bring it up again.

That is until we were in the car together a couple of weeks later and I saw her name pop up on the car's caller ID screen. I asked why she was calling, and he said it was related to the "emergency" she had had before.

Now, if you've read the earlier chapters, you can probably predict what happened next. Yep…Key-Throwing Crazy Bitch surfaced, which led to me getting paranoid, which led to him pulling away, which led to me spying on his parking space. Daily. And, that's not all, of course. I started trying to time my arrival home with his, and I was always on the lookout for him at every intersection close to our community. We continued to see each other, though not as much, and I ignored all the glaring signs the relationship was about to end (I get into this in the next chapter).

During this time, I also finally got a call for a job interview in Phoenix. Before I left I had a conversation with The Digression, and this is where it all went sideways. First of all, you should know after meeting him I considered staying in California. And this was after we'd been seeing each other a month. One month. So now you have an idea of my state of mind before we had our little chit chat. Poor guy. He had no idea what was coming. I told him I was heading to Phoenix for the interview and revealed to him my plan to move back. I told him this made me sad because I really liked him and thought we had something special. He seemed to be sad as well but when he didn't beg, "Please Don't Go!" like I wanted him to, I knew something was up. We decided to talk about it when I got back.

I called him from Phoenix to let him know how it was going, but the conversation was pretty one-sided. Another sign I should have paid more attention to.

I received an offer for the job within a week. I broke the news to him, and he seemed genuinely disappointed. We continued to see each other, but I could feel him pulling away. The more he pulled, the more I clung, and the more crazy my thinking became. I believed we would continue seeing each other, somehow, someway, that we were star-crossed lovers who met at the wrong time, and, I mean, how could the universe do this to us because we were perfect together, and the attraction was so intense, how could this not be the real thing, and why couldn't we figure out a way to stay together and work it out, and, and, and...sigh...(Geez, hot mess)

About this time, my cousin Kim came to visit. Of course I told her all about him, how he was handsome, and he was this, and he was that, and I had finally found the "perfect" guy, and so on, despite the blip with his ex-girlfriend and despite my plan to move back to Phoenix. Now Kim knows me pretty well, and I think she probably suspected I was getting a little ahead of myself with the situation, but of course she graciously listened to me go on and on about this guy.

Her first night in town, we went out to dinner with The Digression. It was a great night, and I thought this was even more "perfect" because he had now met a member of my family. But the next day as Kim and I were leaving the parking lot, I saw the ex-girlfriend's car driving in. It literally took every ounce of discipline for me not to turn around, but Kim and I had a day planned, and I didn't want to ruin it. Of course I ruined the day anyway because she had to listen to me obsess about it ALL day.

We went to a movie that night, but before we left, I couldn't resist taking a peak upstairs to see what car was parked in his spot. I'm sure you'll be shocked to know it was his ex-girlfriend's. I sat there stewing about the situation through the entire movie. I realized he and his ex-girlfriend were never really "over," and when I had given myself permission to sleep with him because they were "over," I had known all along they weren't "over." Please, it had only been a month. I just wanted to have sex with him. I had been played by him, but I had played my part, too. I went over every detail of our relationship during this movie, and by the time we got home and the car was still there, I, once again, snapped. I called him, and when he didn't answer, I left a message full of foul language and unsupported accusations, a message to this day I wish I could delete.

Most guys, when they're done with a relationship, will do their best to just let it fade out and avoid hurting your feelings. At this point I'm sure The Digression was thinking, "Thank God I only have to hang on for a few more weeks."

The last night we were together I somehow knew it would be the last time we saw each other. We had gone to dinner and came back to my place to stay the night. Only he didn't stay. He got up in the middle of the night after we had fallen asleep and went to his own apartment. Ouch. I remember begging him to stay…it was not pretty. I was holding on tightly to something that had already ended, and I knew it. It was like I was having an out of body experience. I watched myself beg him to stay knowing it was the end and saw how pathetic I looked doing it. I wanted to slap myself across the face. What's ironic about that situation was I had pulled the exact same move on him not long after we started sleeping together. I got up in the middle of the night to go to my own apartment, following one of my own rules. But somewhere between then and now I had lost control, and the tables had turned. To make things worse, he left his watch on my nightstand that night and had to come get it the next morning. He picked up the watch and didn't give me a kiss or hug goodbye. That really was the last time I saw him.

Almost immediately I was able to see all the mistakes I had made and how bad my behavior was—how all my old patterns had resurfaced. Looking back now,

I am so disappointed in myself for letting this great opportunity pass me by. The Digression was actually a really great guy. He was a lot of fun, and my last month in L.A. could have been a blast. Instead it was filled with anxiety and remorse. Those last few weeks I literally had to change my schedule so I wouldn't run into him because I was so embarrassed about my behavior.

All the signs were there from the beginning this was meant to be a short, fun, casual encounter and I probably could have saved myself a little heartache had I paid attention. Here's how I knew….

When I met him, he was in a serious relationship with someone…living together serious. That was one sign. For it to end so abruptly and for him to call me just a couple of weeks later, was another sign. For him to tell me it was totally over between the two of them just a short time after I told him I wouldn't sleep with him until it was over…another sign. For me, any kind of intense attraction right off the bat is a sign. The fact that our "relationship" progressed so quickly was a sign. For him to still have the need to be there for his ex-girlfriend was a sign. Me accepting a new job in Phoenix was another sign.

I've often wondered why I digressed so rapidly after I thought I had come so far with casually dating. Only after some time have I finally been able to answer my own question. I lost the control.

Now everyone always gets freaked out with the word control. I never want anyone to think I advocate controlling another person. That is not what I mean. I do however advocate women controlling casual relationships to the benefit of both parties. The woman can control the outcome of every relationship she has. She can control it to be fun and end well. Or, she can control it to be full of drama and end badly. In this case I started out being a fun girl and I gave the impression it would be a fun relationship that would end well. Somewhere in the middle, however, I let Crazy Bitch take control. At that moment I had three choices…I could have allowed her to take control (which I did), I could have just walked away with no drama (better choice), or I could have stayed in the relationship, had lots of fun, all the while knowing it would only last a couple of months because I wanted to move back to Phoenix anyway (best choice).

Bliss Throws Keys:
The End of a Casual Relationship

The end of a casual relationship is where the heart can truly get broken and you can start to lose your mind, especially when he's the one who ends it. This is where you do drive-bys, hack email accounts, look through phones, and throw keys—essentially, you become the worst version of yourself. It sneaks up on you out of nowhere, so you need to watch for it and get a handle on it quickly.

No woman ever sets out to become Key-Throwing Crazy Bitch. You set out to have fun and enjoy the exciting rollercoaster of a new relationship. On some rides, however, somewhere between that first butterfly-inducing drop and the push back into the gate, jarring turns, stomach-churning inversions, and dark tunnels can make the ride seem far more frightening than fun. The good news—or bad, depending on how you look at it—is you're the one operating this roller coaster. You can stop it and get off any time you want. The other side of that coin is when you get thrown off from being jolted around a sharp left turn, it's because you choose to stay in the seat. If you don't like the ride, get off. Or, don't get on in the first place.

This is how it usually went for me: I would meet a guy I wasn't sure I even really liked. He was too tall, too short, too this, too that. He pursued me hard so I would reluctantly give him a chance because you never know, right? I'd start asking my friends: "Do you like him?" "Do you think he's cute?" "Would you go out with him?" Then after about a month or two of dating, I would find myself really liking this guy. I'd realize he was a diamond in the rough and feel so thankful I'd given him a chance. Things would progress and suddenly it would hit me…I had fallen hard for him. And almost instinctively and immediately, he would know he had me. I'd decide to let my guard down a little. He would start pulling away a little, claiming I was putting pressure on him. I'd cling to him, like Crazy Bitch does. He would turn into super jerk and stop communicating with me all together. Then. BAM! There I was again obsessed about a guy I didn't even like to begin with. I'd try to stop seeing him, but would continue to text him, hoping he would realize he missed me and wanted me back. He wouldn't respond. I'd do the old drive by routine and see a strange car in the driveway. I'd lose it and start calling my friends but no one would answer because they were all sick of hearing me talk about this guy. I would retreat into my bedroom for days wondering what happened to me, wondering how I let it get to this point—again! Sound familiar, anyone?

I know it's easier said than done, but in the pages that follow, I teach you how to avoid such a scenario. I offer tips on how to recognize when a relationship is coming to an end (or should be) and how to gracefully exit, even when you're the one being dumped. It's not easy, but you have to take it like a man, honey, and move on….there's no crying in baseball!

The Signs Are Everywhere: How to Recognize When It's Time for a Relationship to End

Follow your first instincts. Feelings are very hard to control, and even harder to stop, especially when they start moving at rollercoaster speeds. You meet a guy who you know isn't right for you, but go out with him anyway for fun. The fun progresses, you spend more and more time together, but deep down you know this ride is just a loop back to the loading zone. Still, you start to like the guy and become attached. And this is where you've gotta break it off. The more time you spend with him, the more likely you are to fall for him. I know you're thinking that may not be such a bad thing, but remember your first instinct? That he wasn't right for you? You knew it in your gut, didn't you? So what's changed? You've spent time together, had some fun and great sex—that's it. Nothing has changed.

Lingering in limbo after three months. If after three months you either don't know where you stand with a guy or don't think you would consider dating him long term, then stop seeing him and move on to the next. There's no reason to waste your time or his by staying. Casual relationships are meant to be short, so unless you think you have truly found someone you want to date more than casually, keep refreshing the bench with new players. If you don't? He will start to expect things from you, or worse, you'll settle and begin to think you're falling in love when you're not.

Stop, look, and listen. If you see you're the one (or becoming the one) always initiating conversation and get-togethers—stop. Let him initiate. If he doesn't, you have your answer. Let it go and move on. If you don't stop initiating things, he will continue to respond and see you when it's convenient for him, but it will be inconsistent and you'll start feeling hurt.

Paper-thin. If he doesn't like your friends, it's because your friends can see right through him. So should you. I know it's hard when you really like a guy, but that's when you're most vulnerable and may not see him for what he is. If he doesn't like your best friends, tries to pit you against them, keeps you from seeing them, or talks bad about them, it's a huge red flag. For one thing, those qualities he despises about your friends he'll eventually see in you and will most likely *require* you to correct to continue seeing him. Two, your friends can see what's going on right away. In fact, I'd bet they saw it the first time they met him. They should be friend enough to say something, and you should be friend enough to listen. Staying in this kind of relationship will eventually drive a wedge between you and all your friends, and then you'll be left with a man who's never satisfied and always trying to change you. In addition, he'll know he can control you—and that's *no bueno*.

Responsibility—Party of One. I hate it when women blame men for being "assholes." Take responsibility for what you are doing rather than blame him for what he's doing. If a guy is trying to control you, leave. If he's abusing you, leave. If he's badmouthing your friends, leave. If he disrespects you, leave. If he makes you feel uncomfortable, leave. If he's blowing you off and not giving you enough attention, leave. If his behavior is in some way causing you stress and anxiety, leave. It's as simple as that.

Red Alert. If there are enough red flags flying around to block the sun, you know better. Get out. You don't need me to tell you what red flags are, although I have given you many examples. If something makes your stomach churn, it's a red flag. Pay attention. Red flags don't go away—they multiply.

Trust yourself. I will admit it's taken me some time to be a pro at this, but you'll get there, I promise. Trusting yourself to walk away from the wrong guy says so much about how you feel about yourself and who you are as a woman. A powerful woman isn't going to sit idly by and let some asshole treat her badly. A powerful woman isn't going to stay in a relationship that's not benefitting her in a positive way. A powerful woman will be able to see the signs and trust her instincts. A powerful woman will listen and act on the advice of her best friends. A powerful woman knows the difference between love and lust. And, finally, my favorite line from the movie *Fried Green Tomatoes* which was chock full of powerful women: "A lady always knows when to leave."

End It Already: How to Break Up and Move On

But, but, but. I would like to sit here and tell you casual dating is always easy. But occasionally when you have to walk away from a guy, it's not. It's especially hard to walk away from the ones you really like. Sometimes even a wonderful and fun relationship still needs to end. You might even think to yourself, "I thought we had something." Well, you did have *something*. You had a fun, brief love affair that is now over. So lick your wounds and move on. Quickly.

It's even more critical for you to walk away from the ones you really like. Those are the relationships that linger on forever because you didn't have the strength to let go months ago when you should have. In these types of relationships, literally out of nowhere, you will suddenly want this guy to be YOURS...and you start hanging on for dear life. Because you didn't end it at the right time, the relationship will almost certainly end in some kind of drama, and most of the time it's the woman causing the drama because she can't let go. Don't be that woman.

Band-Aid. Having a long, drawn out break up in any circumstance is agony. With a casual relationship, it's also ridiculous. Because, really, who the hell cares if it's over? Just end it like ripping off a Band-Aid. Make it short, sweet, and to the point. No drama.

Ignore break-up remorse. This is another trap we get ourselves into. We think, "Did I make the right choice?" "Should I have gone out with him one more time?" "Oh, he looks really good tonight; maybe I should call him tomorrow." Don't suffer from break-up remorse. If he's not calling to tell you he wants to take you out, you made the right choice. If he's not calling to tell you he wants to be with you, you made the right choice. You stepped into your powerful woman suit and told him to take a hike. Now stick to it. You did it for a reason. If nothing else, the fact he's not reaching out to you should give you reason enough. If you want me to be honest, he was probably hoping you'd do the deed so he didn't have to. If you think you might cave and do the 2 a.m. booty call, make a list of all the reasons why you stopped seeing him and keep copies everywhere for quick reference. Keep a copy in your billfold, your car, your make-up bag; shit, keep a copy in your panties if that will help you say no to him when the bar closes.

I am absolutely certain during this period of letting go the guy will resurface or reach out in some sweet way that makes you feel like you've made a huge mistake. It's almost like they can sense you've let go and are starting to heal. Don't fall for it. They just want to know they still have you. Keep the list handy and refer to it often.

Stay strong. I don't think guys have any concept of a casual relationship's timeline. All they know is they like you, like having sex with you, don't intend to marry you, and could go on like that for however long they feel like it. For the most part, they won't be emotionally attached, and they will continue to have a good time with you for as long as you allow it. This is true even after you've stopped seeing each other. The door is always open for him—and why wouldn't it be? You're a fun girl, you guys had a great time together, he let things fizzle out, and you didn't go nuts on him. He might tempt you, and you'll think things have changed, but they haven't. He is just looking for a fun date for that night.

You can't handle the truth. How often does a guy actually sit down to tell you he's really enjoyed spending time with you, but that he just doesn't think it's going to work out? I can answer that. NEVER. More than likely he will stop calling, stop responding to texts, unfriend you on Facebook, and find another Starbucks route. Or, he'll start acting like a super jerk, so *you'll* break up with *him*. Most guys avoid confrontation at all costs. Why? Because Crazy Bitch can surface in *any* woman! Women are Crazy Bitches! They cry, they yell, they manipulate men into giving it another couple of weeks, they use sex to keep control, and so on. Women are masters at squeezing every last drop out of a relationship. Most guys are not equipped with the gene to end relationships by calling you up and telling you how awesome you are, how much fun they had with you, how lucky the next guy will be, and how they think it's best for you to part ways on a high note. So if you're lucky enough to have a guy sit you down and tell you the truth, don't make it scary for him. It's closed. Don't make him turn into an asshole. Be gracious, be thankful he gave it to you straight, and move on. Then go take out your frustrations at CrossFit.

Closure. Speaking of closed, what is it with women and "closure"? No, seriously! "I could move on, but I just need some sort of closure." "I'm fine, but I just need closure." Blah, blah, blah. All you are looking for is another excuse to call, see, or sleep with him one last time, to essentially hang on for dear life until he has no choice but to treat you like shit so you will move on. Don't worry about getting closure. If he stops communicating—it's closed.

Hold your calls. I love this one. You decide you don't want to see a guy anymore, or he decides he doesn't want to see you. You exchange heated words, and in the moment, you say, "Don't call me again!" Then, when he doesn't call, you're pissed. If he isn't calling you, it doesn't mean he is at home pining over you in agony, dying to call you but can't because you told him not to. It means he's moved on, and so should you. Refer back to earlier communication tips.

Happy Birthday means...Happy Birthday. A text on your birthday after you've stopped seeing someone doesn't mean, "I miss you and I can't live without you." It means, "Happy birthday." Same goes for holidays and for texts about "special days" you guys shared. Just because he's having a reminiscent moment doesn't mean you should assume he's trying to get back with you. It means something reminded him of you, and he wanted you to know. That's it.

Now on the other hand, you should never text or call him on his birthday or holidays because he will interpret that as drama and will think you're trying to get back together.

Get over yourself. A few tender moments and good sex are not enough to build a future on. Don't fall into the trap of confusing infatuation with love. They are two very different things. Just because a guy spent a little time with you, revealed a little of himself to you, made you feel like a hot tamale in bed, and took you on a few trips doesn't mean he fell in love. It means he liked you enough to see you more than once. You had some good times. Leave it at that. He may call after a few weeks, after a few months, or after a few years. If he does, and you're free to entertain him, then go for it. Just remember what it was—and what it's not.

Doubting yourself. Sometimes you will be the one walking away (hopefully most of the time), and sometimes he will be the one walking away. The more this happens, the more you will start to doubt yourself or question your worth. Feel the feeling. Then…Let. It. Go. You are fine. Everything is fine.

11

Interpreting Guy Behavior

Okay, girls, following are a few generalizations about men and mostly pertain to those you've only been seeing a short time. Just know, though, my observations and interpretations are a result of lots and lots of actual experience.

Understanding Guy Communication

"I love you," is a fatal phrase if it comes from a guy you have only been seeing for a few weeks. Why? Chances are he's trying to get into your pants if he hasn't already. Or, he's one of those guys that falls fast and leaves fast. Or, he may actually be in love with you, in which case, I'd be very cautious. He could turn into a stalker.

"Let's stay in and watch a movie," is code for "Let's watch the movie for the first 15 minutes, then have sex." If you're not prepared for the advances, tell him, "I'm not ready for 'movie night,'" and he will get the hint. If he never calls you again, take it as a compliment: he thought enough of you not to string you along. That actually happened to me with a guy I had just met in a club in L.A. We exchanged numbers,

and he called me a few days later to see if I wanted to hang out. His suggestion? Come over and watch a movie. I told him, "I'm not ready for movie night." Guess what? He never called again. I called him a few weeks later to see if he wanted to get together, and he actually said to me, "I get the feeling you're more into dating someone, and I'm more into hooking up. If you're down with that, then cool, I'd love to get together." At first, I was taken aback and thought, "What an asshole." My second thought, though, was "What a gift." This guy could have led me on for a few dates with one end in mind, but he didn't. He gave it to me straight. He saved me a possible heartache, and I didn't make it scary for him. I took it like a lady and thanked him for being honest.

"I just want to cuddle," is code for "I'm going to try at least three times to have sex with you." Again, if you're sleeping over with a guy, you'd better expect him to try something. He's playing Mr. Nice Guy so you'll stay. It's his last ditch effort to get you into his territory. Don't fall for it. Either be prepared to ward off his advances and piss him off, or be prepared for how you'll feel the morning after you gave in and had sex with him. Neither one feels good. Alternatively, you could do what I do: offer him a Xanax and knock his ass out.

"I fell asleep," is code for "I decided to go out with someone else tonight." Actually, this phrase could be code for many things, none of which is good. The fact is he doesn't want to see you. For whatever reason, he didn't have enough balls to call and tell you that. Let's say he did want to take a nap. If you were important enough, he would have set his alarm.

"I didn't get your text," is code for "I saw your text but decided not to respond." Guys hang themselves on this one within the first few dates. Don't they realize we observe their phone checking and texting habits immediately and commit them to memory? You know he got your text. You know he saw your text. Let's say he did by some chance miss your text. If he really was interested in you, he would have texted you to say, "Hey, are we still on for tonight?" or "Hey, why haven't you texted me?"

Grand gestures don't mean a thing, either. Like taking an afternoon flight to come see you. Inviting you away for the weekend. Sending you a ticket to come see him. Blowing everyone else off, including work, so he can spend the afternoon with you. Spending $225 on a taxi across the desert so you can be together. All of this means nothing. Except he's horny and likes you enough to make the effort this one time. It may never happen again so enjoy it while it lasts.

"I don't want to hurt you," is code for 1) I've met someone else I like better; 2) I think you're a great girl but just not the right girl for me; 3) you're getting too close; or 4) this has been fun, but now it's time to move on.

Two statements to especially look out for: *"I just want to hook up"* and *"I'm not looking for anything serious."* These two statements mean, "I just want to hook up" and "I'm not looking for anything serious." If you still sleep with a guy who says either of these, then no complaining when he never calls you again. This goes along with taking responsibility for your actions, girls. He told you he was just looking for a hook up, so why did you sleep with him? He picked you up at 1 a.m. as the bar was closing, so what did you expect? Did you think you were so amazing in bed that it would change his mind? If you're down for just a hook up, then awesome, go for it. If you're expecting anything to happen beyond that night, you're a fool.

If a man starts talking about his ex, run. Either he's still in love with her, he's still seeing her on the side, she really broke his heart, or he's comparing you to her. Any of these examples are nothing you want to deal with, so get the hell out and fast.

My last reminder on communication (and we've all heard this before): Actions, of course, always speak louder than words.

Understanding Guy Actions

In casual dating, you are the one who needs to be in control, not him. If you let him take control, you're two bus stops and one train away from the land of heartbreak. All he wants to do is have fun and make you happy, but when things start changing for you emotionally, he won't know what to do. He'll inadvertently end up hurting you. It's best to let him follow you, which should be down the road of fun and adventure with no expectations.

If you tell him what you're looking for, and he blows you off, that's his way of telling you he can't give you what you want right now. Don't take it personally. Move on. Don't change what you're looking for to fit what he can give—big mistake! You're compromising already and you've only been hanging out with the guy a couple of weeks? Check yourself. He's not a jerk—he's just not the guy for you at this time.

Speaking of jerks, I'll go ahead and tell you most guys don't set out to be jerks. It's just that most girls give them no choice. For example, he told you he just wanted to hook up, but you kept calling. He told you he wasn't interested in a serious relationship, but you kept pressuring him. He tried in so many ways (actions, actions, actions) to let you know you're not the one for him, but you kept hanging around. He hasn't reached out to you in months, but you keep texting him. He told you he couldn't meet up, you drove by his house to see if he was with another girl, and he saw you. He told you he was going out with his friends, and you showed up at the same place with your girlfriends. Get my drift? Tell Crazy Bitch to go crash some else's party, and move on!

If you are lucky enough to find a guy who will end the relationship before you have to, thank him! He's acting like a decent guy and doing you a favor.

All men have a pattern of behavior—like the cell phone thing I mentioned earlier. Don't they realize we know they check their phone every five minutes? Like he didn't get my text. Whatever. In the beginning of a casual relationship, the patterns will emerge. Pay attention. When you see him start to break his pattern of behavior, whatever behavior it is, something's up.

Start preparing for the end.

I've talked a lot about men and their behaviors in this chapter, but I may have left you wondering, how to distinguish the bullshit from the truth? In casual dating, there is no difference. The bullshit is the truth. Don't fall for it.

A typical guy timeline for casual dating goes a little like this. The two of you meet in however form or fashion and he gets your number. He's all into you because this is new to him. You spend lots of quality time together, you have lots of sex, you talk about future plans, you start to get a little comfortable, then about one to two months in there's a shift. He still really likes you and keeps seeing you but probably not quite as often. He starts thinking about how he's going to phase the relationship out and is praying you won't make a big deal out of it. He starts pulling away little by little. If he's lucky you just pull away too, and that's that. Or, if he's lucky, the relationship lingers for a while because he actually does like you, wants to be able to use you as the occasional booty call, and is again, hoping you won't make a big deal of it. If he's not lucky, neither of these options play out and it's awkward for the next several months until the relationship finally ends with some kind of drama.

There are all sorts of reasons why guys pull away. They get bored. They meet someone new. They get busy with work. They don't want to feel like they're tied down. The relationship gets too serious. They just want the fun and when the intimacy enters the relationship, they panic. You were just a conquest. There's too much drama. They don't like cats. They are into dating around. You're always too busy. You're too young or too old. They're focused on whatever personal goals they have and you're getting in the way. Whatever. My point is….none of this really has anything to do with you. You don't need to worry about why he's pulling away. And you cannot take it personally when a guy starts to pull away. Don't try reading into it wondering what you should have done differently. You shouldn't have done anything differently. It is what it is. You have to let it go.

Understanding Guy Types

The Broken Man
We've all come across that "broken" man. You know the type. His ex really did a number on him, he's told you all about it (his side of the story at least), he's led you to believe he's given up on love, etc. A couple of things could be going on here. 1) He's playing into your emotions, and once he has you, he will have won,

and the game will be over. 2) He really is broken. If that's the case, you're not a mechanic, so don't try to fix him. He needs to fix himself, then give you a call. It's not your job to help heal a man from whatever. Let some other woman do it. You don't need another project in your life. It's a lot of work, and you get absolutely no benefit whatsoever. Trust me, once he's fixed, he'll move on to someone else, and you'll be left wondering what the hell just happened.

The Representative

Understand the guy you see for the first few months isn't the real guy at all. That's another reason not to get too excited about someone for at least six months. By that time (if you're still hanging out), the representative is tired of campaigning and just wants to get laid without making a big production out of it.

Mr. Notoriety

If he has acted a certain way with one woman, he will act the same with you, too. You will not be the exception. You will not be the one to inspire him to change his ways. I always see this happen when you're initially in the "friend zone" with a guy. You see how he treats women, yet you expect him to treat you differently. I also see this when you're dating someone a friend of a friend has dated. You've heard all the stories, but you think it will be different with you because that other girl was crazy. Not so. Not so. If you think you're special, you're not. If you think you can change him, you can't. Also, if someone (especially another woman) tells you a bad story about the guy you are dating, you should probably believe it and stop seeing him immediately. Most women (especially good friends) have no reason to lie to you, so as much as it pains you to hear what she has to say, listen and take action.

The Blame Game Trophy Holder

Some guys are really good at turning things around and making it your fault. Let them, and then break it off. It's not worth it to argue, and it's just a way for them to gain control. This is the worst kind of manipulation by a man, and it's the most detrimental to a woman. I see so many women fall into low self-esteem because the man they're dating won't take responsibility for his actions. In casual relationships, it's not even worth it to go down this road. Cut ties while it's still early, and be thankful you got out when you did.

The Defendant

He is guilty until proven innocent, and even then proceed with caution. If you find something while "looking around" that causes you to question his integrity or morality, stop seeing him immediately. You do not owe him an explanation.

The It's-All-Fun-and-Games Guy

You are a game to him, so let him play you. Don't get involved emotionally, and just enjoy it! Play back! This is a time when you're supposed to be having fun, trying new things, and stepping out of your comfort zone. Have a blast, but keep your emotions in check. And exit gracefully when the fun is over.

The Sheep-Clad Wolf

A ton of guys out there like to play themselves off as "Mr. Nice Guy." These are the worst kind of men. They put on a show for you from the beginning, likely telling you a sad story to appeal to your sensitive nature. If you didn't already know, there are courses out there to help guys score chicks, and this is the type of guy who has done his research. Men use all kinds of tricks and tactics to further their game, and truly, we don't want to know what they are—because we like 'em! The polite manners, the well-planned compliments, the gazes of affection, the soft, gentle caress of your body. Don't be naïve. Be smart and conduct proper due diligence before you just hop into bed with a guy—unless that's all you're after, too.

The Barrier Breaker

Beware of the guy trying to break down your wall. He's in it for one reason and one reason only: to win. Believe it or not, some men out there see a strong woman who's in control and immediately see a huge (enticing) challenge. To make matters worse, when he realizes you have dating savvy, he'll try even harder to break you. Once you've let the wall down, he's out.

The Funny Guy

Watch out for the funny guy...he gets laid—plenty. Trust me. Those of you who love funny guys know exactly what I mean. The Prelude was the funniest guy I'd ever met, and he knew making a woman laugh would get his foot in the door immediately. The funny guy who knows how to work it can—and will—get ANY woman he wants. I'm not saying you should avoid them all together, but I am saying watch out. Funny guys may not be the best looking. You may even think you're doing them a favor by going home with them. But make no mistake; it won't be funny later when you realize he's never going to call you again.

The Bad Boy

Now you know I love bad boys—always have. You have only one option here: buckle in tight and enjoy the ride while it lasts. Just remember to keep the end in mind when you start out. Trust me, the pleasure far outweighs the pain, so just go for it.

The Married Man

Regardless of what you may think, married men are not safe to date. If you think you can just have sex with a married man with no emotional attachment, you can't. You are much more susceptible to falling hard because you think he's "safe." You let your guard down, you relinquish a little control here and there, and before you know it, you're in so deep you can't breathe. Married men have the same capacity to hurt you as any other men do. In fact, they're more experienced at it. He got you to agree so easily to a betrayal, didn't he?

For a while in my twenties, I thought married men were the perfect men to date. They're fun. They're exciting. The sex is outstanding. They make you feel like you're so special, buy you gifts, take you on trips, leave you passionate messages, and send you hot texts. You get only the good and none of the bad. Sounds amazing, right? Wrong. Aside from the major fact you're betraying another woman, you'll end up betraying yourself. It will get the better of you—it's just a matter of time.

The Master

Beware The Master. You remember him, don't you? The inspiration for this book? So many men out there will seduce you. They may not set out to hurt you, but more than likely, they can't help themselves. It's their pattern, just like you have yours.

12

Houston...We have a Problem: Keeping Your Dignity

This chapter is perhaps the most important in the book. After a relationship ends, any normal girl can go from calm to crazy in about .0267 seconds. If you don't take any other of my advice, take the advice in this chapter. Otherwise, you might be the next featured girl on www.shesacrazybitch.com. Following are several scenarios when a woman can quickly lose her dignity.

Women lose their dignity when...

...they compromise their own moral integrity. To each her own on this one. What's immoral to one may not be to another, so you need to evaluate what this means for you. Figure out your boundaries, and don't cross them—for any man.

...they let men hurt them. Like I said before, if a man insults you, belittles you, disrespects you, embarrasses you, makes fun of you, or treats you in any way that makes you feel bad, stop seeing him immediately. Period. No exceptions and no explanations needed. Just stop taking his calls. This type of guy is a master at controlling women, and he will find a way to guilt you back into seeing him again. Don't fall for it. It's a trap. His behavior will only get worse and worse as time goes on.

...they allow bad patterns of behavior to continue. If he doesn't call, doesn't show up, or doesn't follow through on whatever he said he was going to do and it matters to you, stop seeing him. If you're casually dating, though, and have a nice, full bench, then this type of behavior won't matter as much. In that case, you just respond in kind. Cancel at the last minute, don't return his calls, whatever. Treat him like he's treating you. No one cares, no one's feelings are getting hurt, and everyone is happy.

...they stay around too long. You know it's not working. He knows it's not working. The fun is over. He's not calling you as often as he was. You've caught him in a few lies. He's turned into a super jerk. You see his posts on Facebook with other women. All of these are clear indications it's time to go. As my friend Jean says, "It's time to take your pride while it's still intact and leave."

...they snoop around. Don't let this be confused with the "look around a little" tip I gave you in the beginning. A jealous woman does better research than the FBI, so you need to know where to draw the line. Going beyond a little sneak-a-peek here and there is a problem. Once you start looking into his call logs, text logs, emails, drawers, it won't stop. You've gone way past casual at this point, and it's time to get a grip. If you feel the need to look, don't. Instead, ask yourself why you're snooping. Most likely, the answer will reveal an insecurity of yours that needs to be handled. Otherwise, you have reason not to trust him and therefore have reason not to date him anyway.

...try to get "closure." What possible amount of good can come out of you trying to get closure? None, I tell you. None. What more is there for you to know? He doesn't want to date you any longer. If he didn't tell you why, then he doesn't want to tell you why. Do you really want to know why? Really? Do you really want to torture yourself further? That's what it boils down to, in my opinion. Women love pain. Some revel in it. I can't stand it when women have to get closure. Closure for what? It's over. Move on.

...they continue to communicate after it's over. Be strong: don't call. When it's over, it's over. I know it's super hard not to call, or text, or Facebook, or email, or send a carrier pigeon, but you must refrain.

If he's the one who pulled away or dumped you, it's even more critical for you to move on. He isn't calling you, you know he's out with other girls, and he's not responding to your attempts to see him. Don't call or text him. He doesn't want you back. If he did, he'd call. You're not going to get the answer you're looking for when you call, so why subject yourself to further humiliation?

If you dumped him, then refer back to the "breakup remorse" tip. There was a reason you let him go. Just because you see him out with some new hot chick doesn't mean he's suddenly attractive again. Remember, she'll be dealing with all the crap you dealt with before too long. Again, no reason to call.

One sure-fire way to avoid this is to perform a phone number exorcism. I've done it many, many times and almost instantly regretted it every time. But then in almost just as short of time, I'm thankful I did it. If you don't have the strength to do this, have a friend do it for you. If you don't have the strength to ask a friend to do it for you, then at least change his name in your phone to something that will remind you every time he calls how he made you feel. If you can't think of something clever, try "Dignity." That should suffice. My friend Char did this, and whenever "Dignity" called, she was usually able to let the call go to voice mail. This gave her time to think and choose her next step without the rush of feelings clouding her judgment.

...they send "I miss you" texts. This goes along with the "no communicating after it's over" rule, but I separate it out for a reason. Women think that sending the "I miss you" text will spark some feeling in the guy and make him remember how good you were together. It won't. You're not going to get the response you're looking for, so why hurt yourself intentionally? Oh yeah, I forgot. Women love pain.

...they do drive-bys. I know you want to, and you've done it before. So have I. Nevertheless, I don't do them anymore. Why? I learned my lesson. Worst-case scenario? He catches you driving by. It will only further validate why he dumped you in the first place. But your dignity is at stake here whether he sees you or not. Think about what you're doing: You're driving by a guy's house you used to date to see...what? What will you gain from seeing him there with someone else? Validation? For what? That he can't live without you? Obviously not. That he can't move on? Again, not. That he made the wrong choice in letting you go? Clearly not, because you've been replaced by Crazy Bitch who's doing midnight drive-bys.

...they think "sex once more" will win him back. It won't. This tactic will only leave him feeling satisfied and you feeling like a hooker. Blunt, I know, but this one is terrible for a woman's self-esteem and has no chance of ending well. Let's say it does spark the relationship again. It will only be for a little while. I guarantee he doesn't want to get back with you long term. As I said before, if he did, he'd be calling you, and not at 2 a.m. for a booty call. If you called him at 2 a.m. for a booty call, and it's blowing up in your face now, then I don't feel sorry for you.

...they try to make a point. Remember my stellar throwing keys moment? This is how that entire mess started. I was so pissed I'd been stood up I went straight to his apartment to make a point: How dare he stand me up. Right. Enter Crazy Bitch. Looking back now, I lost my dignity way before this point, and he knew it. He just kept me around to toy with me because he could—and I let him.

13

Calling in for Backup: Knowing When You Need an Intervention

Sometimes our judgment gets so clouded we lose all control and no longer have the capacity to make decisions for ourselves. This is where your friends come in. Now, more than ever, you have to listen to what they are saying. More importantly, do what they tell you to do.

A couple of signs to look out for:

- You keep hearing the same feedback from different sets of friends.
- You've lost the support of your friends.
- You keep going back to this guy even after your friends have told you not to.
- You talk about him constantly when you're supposed to be having fun with your friends.
- When this guy calls you at the last minute wanting to hang out (probably because you were his 2nd or 3rd choice and no one else was free), you cancel your plans with friends immediately to accommodate him.
- You've alienated your friends one by one, and

now no one wants to hang out with you anymore, except...

- ...the few friends who, 1) don't really care enough about you to tell you the truth, 2) are using you for some unknown reason, or 3) have been around so long nothing will rattle the friendship at this point.

If you've gotten to this point, your friends may have to step in, sit you down, and have a heart-to-heart. I would hope, after all I've taught you, you'd no longer end up at this point. But if not, this should be a great lesson for you. No man is worth losing yourself or your friends over. No man.

Being able to recognize you need an intervention is a gift. It takes a strong woman to admit this to herself and to her friends. Openly confessing your needs to your friends will help them hold you accountable for your actions and give them a chance to step up and really be a friend to you.

If you feel yourself losing control, don't see him or communicate with him for at least two weeks. I can always feel it when the control switch shuts off in my psyche. Perhaps an action I used to be okay with suddenly is not okay. For example: I used to be okay with him taking his time to respond to my texts, but now I'm not okay with it. I used to be okay with both of us dating a bunch of people, but now I get super jealous if I find out any details. I used to be okay with no expectations; now I expect everything. I used to be the fun, flirty, hot girl, but now I'm acting needy and bitchy. I used to take one route to work, but now I go 30 minutes out of my way so I can drive by his house. I know for certain at this point if I stay in this any longer, there's a huge heartache in store for me.

This invariably happens when I'm dating someone I absolutely know is not right for me. It starts out fun, the two of us have a great time and great sex with no strings attached, no expectations, and I try to keep the end in mind. But the more time we spend together, the more I like him, and the more I start making up shit…and then suddenly, I've passed the point of no return. I'm not saying I come to the point where I think this guy *could* be "the one." I knew from the get-go that wasn't a possibility. I'm saying I start to feel like I could *make* him "the one." See the difference? Giving yourself a break from the situation will help you see it clearly. During this time, talk to your friends, get back to doing the things you love, clear your mind, refocus your energy, and start building the bench back up.

14

Stop, Drop, and Roll:
Knowing when to walk away

When you see a sign a man is not honorable in any way, shape, or form, walk away. Disrespectfulness, unkindness, dishonorableness—these are character flaws you cannot change. No matter how much chemistry you have, honor and respect are essential qualities of any man. In my opinion, any man who lies, cheats, steals, abuses animals or children, talks badly about his ex-girlfriends, is carelessly irresponsible with money, constantly cancels plans at the last minute, etc. is not worth one minute of your time. Before you invest one more second, walk away.

Dishonorableness is a no brainer, but other red flags may not be so high-flying. Maybe, for example, he's not a bad guy, but for whatever reason, deep down you knew he wasn't right for you from the beginning. You've let enough time pass, and you instinctively know you've been forcing it. You've had some fun, gained some new experiences, possibly made a great running buddy, but it's time to move past the romance. Chances are he feels it, too. But most guys want to avoid confrontation, so they will just keep seeing you. Or, they want to keep you on the hook as a casual booty call. Most of you instinctively already know this but choose to ignore the situation and hope it goes away on its own. It won't. It will get worse. Rather than waiting for a guy to admit it's over, or "making" a guy turn into super jerk, just move on.

We've talked about this a little already, but let me reiterate. He used to respond to your text messages right away. Suddenly (or not so suddenly), it's taking him hours or days to return your texts. You still see him check his phone every five minutes when he's with you, so you know he hasn't turned over some new anti-technology leaf. If you've not already established it's not necessary to respond to you right away, there's a problem.

But remember, this is a casual relationship. You don't have to make a big scene about it. Just pull back on the communication a bit, and see what happens. If he pulls back even more, you know you're making the right decision. Let the relationship fade. There's no need to analyze what's going on or try to understand what went wrong. Just move on. If he resurfaces in a few months and you feel like seeing him, then go for it! Personally, I try not to initiate conversation, but if a guy reaches out to me, I will respond and see him, but only if I am confident I can be the fun, flirty, hot girl with no drama and no expectations.

Casual dating takes practice, and in the beginning, you may not trust yourself to choose the right guy. That's to be expected. You do, however, need to trust yourself enough to walk away from the wrong guy at the right time. You'll know the right time. We've talked about a lot of scenarios. Just pay attention to what's going on and remember the following: In casual dating you should always listen to your head, not your heart.

When you tell a guy you don't want to see him anymore, don't explain. Just say, "I don't think we are a good fit for each other." Leave the relationship with integrity and grace—no drama and no blame. Look, no one likes this situation. He doesn't like hearing it, and you don't like saying it. If you want to be a bit gentler, tell him you've rekindled with an old flame. This way he doesn't feel like it's about him, and more than likely you could remain friends. Most of the time I just limit communication until the relationship eventually fizzles out. Rarely do I have a guy ask me for an explanation.

Don't romanticize the relationship. It was what it was, and now it is what it is: over. You have to respect and love yourself enough to walk away the minute you realize it.

Finally, sometimes you have to be willing to walk away from a "really great guy" for the sake of your well-being. Maybe this isn't the right time for you to be dating. Maybe you've just come out of a serious relationship. Maybe you just need to be alone for a while. I know so many women who can't be alone. They move from one relationship to another, avoiding the issues internally that need to be dealt with. Take a chance and date yourself for a while. It might end up being the best relationship you've ever had!

15

Bliss Finds Her Way Back: What to do When It's Over

Ultimately, as I've said, in casual dating relationships it's best to leave on a high note, if possible. This is supposed to have been a fun experience that's maybe also taught you a thing or two about yourself and men. You've ended it at the appropriate time to avoid getting hurt or hurting him. Feel good about the time you've spent together, and see the gifts the relationship brought you.

In order to successfully end a casual relationship, keep these tips in mind:

It's okay to mourn the loss of a casual relationship, especially the ones where you really liked the guy. If you're anything like me, you decided to go for it, you had a ton of fun, but now it's over, and it hurts a little. Give yourself some time to mourn, but not too much time. I'm talking a couple of weeks tops. Then pick yourself up and keep going.

Keep the bench full at all times. When something ends with one guy, you have another one or two to hang out with. No biggie.

Realize when it's necessary to perform the exorcism, then follow through with it. Solicit help from friends if needed, and then do it. Just like ripping off a Band-Aid—you have to let the wound breathe so it can heal.

I hope your casual relationships end amicably, but if one doesn't, don't be afraid to teach someone a lesson. You have nothing to lose right now, and the advice you give a guy could be the one thing that straightens him out. If it's something that shouldn't go unsaid, then say it. Just make sure what's being said isn't coming from a place of pain and revenge. It has to come from a place of honesty and respect. And don't over-do it. Make your point then drop it. The same goes for the guy if he has something to say to you. Take it like a powerful woman: Thank him for his honesty, and move on.

On that same note, don't feel like you have to have the last word. Women love having the last word. Especially don't use drama or anger as an excuse to communicate with him. It's too late to make a stand. Your last few words of adoration or anger won't matter. There is no need to get the last word. Just let it go.

Distance yourself from his friends or any mutual business acquaintances, at least for the time being.

In a month or so, you'll be over it, and everything can go back to normal.

Make sure your friends know the boundaries. Should they tell you if they see him, or should they keep it to themselves? Ask yourself if you're prepared to know. What if they see him with another girl? Do you want to know? All of this is totally up to you; you have to decide what you can and cannot take. However, if you tell your friends not to tell you and then find out later they saw him, you can't get upset. They were only abiding by your wishes. By the same token, if you tell them to tell you, you can't get upset about what they tell you. You asked for it. My friends are pretty trained by now…they know if I'm trying to end it with a guy, they are absolutely forbidden from interacting with him on Facebook for the time being. And they know not to talk about this guy until I tell them it's okay. Now if I've told my friends the topic of this guy is off limits, and I bring his name up in conversation, then they have the right to cut me off and shut me up immediately.

Beware of thoughts like, "But I really liked him," and "I really thought we had something." You did have something: a casual relationship. It was fun, exciting, passionate, like nothing you've ever felt before. Well, it's over now, so move on, and take the lesson with you. And, if you catch yourself saying, "He was perfect for me," stop. Really? Was he? You had some fun and a few tender moments. That doesn't make him perfect for you. If he was so perfect for you, then why did it only last for three months? Keep it in perspective.

All you need to do is get through one more hour. Then get through one more day. Then get through one more week. Trust that you made the right choice. As my friend Steph says "One day you'll wake up, and he just won't smell good anymore." And that, my friends, is a great day.

Go out, and have some fun! There is no better way to give yourself a boost than to dress up and go out on the town. It doesn't hurt to have a big smile on your face and lots of cute boys around. I have a play list on my iPod that gets a lot of use when I'm down. I put songs on there I know will lift my spirits. I also get lots of rest and force myself to work out. It's hard not to escape into a bottle of tequila, but that only makes matters worse for me. I know it's really, really hard. But try to have a little piece of fun every day until you're back 100 percent.

More on the "closure" thing. Unless it's an heirloom

piece of family jewelry, leave it behind. If you left something behind on purpose so you would get to see him one more time—shame on you!

Don't let remorse make you do something stupid like the 2 a.m. booty call we already talked about. Get in a cab, go home, and immediately take a sleeping pill so you'll pass out before you have the chance to text him.

Get ahold of yourself, and just stop. Stop gazing at his picture, stop listening to that one voice mail you saved, stop reading *his* horoscope, stop fantasizing about him (and by fantasizing, you know what I mean), stop driving by his house, stop going to his website, stop playing the song over and over again that reminds you of him. Just stay away from Facebook, Instagram, Pinterest, Linked In, and Google. Stop following him on Twitter, wash the pillow case that has his smell all over it. Seriously, get a grip, and just stop.

Speaking of fantasizing—you have to mix it up in your head, and think of other things besides him when you're...you know...having a moment. Find something else to give your mind inspiration because if you keep thinking about him, it's like he's still in your life. And he's not. The sooner you let go physically the better.

Delete all the pictures you have stored of him on your phone and your computer, or at least file them away where you cannot see them every time you open your picture folder. No, scratch that. Delete them. Unless it's a cute picture of you, then crop it, Photoshop it, and save it before you delete the original.

Don't call, text, or email without getting at least two other opinions, preferably from your "grounded" friends, who are going to tell you not to. It is going to drive you nuts, but don't do it. What are you trying to accomplish by calling or texting? What are your motives? Is there a pattern of behavior here for you to observe and correct? Once you hit the send button, I one-hundred-percent guarantee you'll immediately regret whatever it was you said. Just walk away from your phone or computer for a while before that happens.

If you were really into a guy who you had a good three-month run with that blew up at the end, you're going to have good and bad days for a while. The worst is yet to come as things really sink in. Just be prepared for it, and have a plan for when days like that hit you. Keep a stash of Xanax on hand. It sounds like I'm a drug pusher, but seriously, sometimes you just need it.

Try not to fall into the "I'm so stupid" way of thinking. It's so easy for us to start blaming ourselves for making the same mistakes. It's okay to make mistakes, as long as you eventually see the pattern and do something about it.

Learn to love being alone, and don't be afraid to be alone. I'm serious when I tell you: being alone is so amazing. There is nothing more powerful than being totally in control of your own life and your own happiness.

If all else fails, move. No, seriously. I did that once. Okay, maybe twice.

16

Stages of the Game: Three Dating Scenarios—Revisited

Remember the three scenarios we went through in the beginning? It's time for us to revisit those now with all the things you've learned.

Week 1

Scenario 1: You met a cute guy who doesn't exactly fit what you think your "type" is. You decide, what the hell, and give him your number anyway. He calls you two days later to set up a date. You're kind of excited because it's always exiting to begin a new casual relationship. With the end in mind, you dive in and have fun while it lasts!

Scenario 2: You met the *perfect* guy and exchanged numbers. He called to ask you out for Saturday night. You know no one can be this perfect, so you move forward with caution, realizing his true colors will come out pretty quickly.

Scenario 3: You met a super-hot, total bad boy while out with your friends, got drunk, and went home with him. The next morning you're hoping he doesn't ask you out for breakfast because you have a major date planned for that night, and you need all day to prepare.

Weeks 2 – 4

Scenario 1: You've been on a couple of dates, but as suspected there's no spark. You decide to keep hanging out with him because you've discovered he's the perfect guy for certain occasions. Let's continue to call him Steady Eddie.

Scenario 2: You've gone out once with Mr. Perfect, and at first glance he's, yep, perfect. He's charming, funny, successful, gorgeous—and a gentleman. He didn't even try to kiss you, but you know this is a game he plays to win women over. And he's good at it. You can see him being a blast around your friends, but there's no way you're introducing him to anyone, especially not your mom. You need to play this one out awhile and see what happens.

Scenario 3: You met up with Bad Boy Bill for happy hour on Friday night and didn't come up for air until Saturday afternoon. This didn't change from the original scenario. Duh.

Month 2

Scenario 1: Steady Eddie has proven to be a great running buddy. You've also gone hiking, clubbing, out to the movies, and out to dinner a few times—you share a lot of interests. Your cousin's wedding was bearable with him around, and like I said before, the sex wasn't half bad. You decide you like this guy but have no expectations.

Scenario 2: Mr. Perfect is fun, fun, fun. Nice dinners and weekend trips. Little gifts here and there. You're eating it up! He gives you his undivided attention when you're together, and you have great conversation. You look forward to the next date, but you don't expect the next date. The holidays are coming up, and you know you probably won't see him much because you'll be busy with your friends and family. No biggie.

Scenario 3: You're still having a great time with Bad Boy Bill. You both text each other whenever it's convenient and get together here and there. It's nice to have a steady booty call. He's so hot.

Month 3

Scenario 1: You're hanging out with Steady Eddie a lot. You know he's seeing other girls, and he knows you're seeing other guys. So far, not a problem. The sex has gotten better with time, and you realize you really like this guy. BUT, you're also enjoying dating around more and don't want to be tied down to anyone.

Scenario 2: Mr. Perfect is MIA. It's been two weeks since you've seen him. You've exchanged texts and voice mails, but you can't seem to get your schedules together. The holidays are coming up, so it's not that big of a deal…you'll see him next year.

Scenario 3: You run into Bad Boy Bill one night at the club, and he gives you a wink over the shoulder of the hot blonde he's got his arm around. You panic a little because you've got your eye on someone else at the bar, and you don't want Bad Boy Bill to see you with another guy…hate to ruin a solid booty call. You see him later that night at another club, and he's alone. You guys chat it up for a while, have a hot make-out session in the corner, then go off with your respective friends. You're hoping he doesn't text you later because you kinda want to hook up with this other guy. The club closes and no text from Bad Boy Bill…you're in the clear!

Months 4 – 5

Scenario 1: Steady Eddie can't figure you out. You

seem really into him, but you're not up his ass like most women are. He likes that you go with the flow and have remained a fun, cool chick to hang out with. You're not really what he's looking for, but he enjoys hanging out with you and will continue doing so until whenever!

Scenario 2: You haven't seen Mr. Perfect since before the holidays, and now it's almost February. You already know the reason… Mr. Perfect seduced you then stopped calling when he got bored. You knew this about him when you met him, but decided to proceed with caution anyway. You had a great time, enjoyed being showered with attention and gifts, and yesterday you met someone even more perfect to hang with for a few months!

Scenario 3: Bad Boy Bill sends you a random text every now and then, but most of the time you don't respond. You know he's only doing it to make sure you're still on the hook. It's cool if you run into each other, and you may get together every few months. The two of you are Facebook friends and keep up with each other that way. He's always got some new hot chick on his arm, but you don't really care. You've got hot guys on your arm all the time…AND your smart enough not to post that shit on Facebook.

The Finale

The Finale

This last dating story pretty well sums up everything I've talked about in my book. While overall, I think I handled things pretty well and according to my own dating philosophies, I admit I still made some mistakes. BUT, I also recognized what I was doing in the moment—I made every choice with my eyes wide open and fully aware of the likely consequences. I never lost control.

It was August in Phoenix, and I was out late one night at W Hotel when I met The Finale. I was by myself because all my friends had ditched me for dudes. It happens.

While aimlessly walking through the crowd, The Finale reached out and grabbed me by the arm. I spun around thinking, "Who the hell has the nerve to—" But when I saw him, I didn't care so much. He was clearly about 15 (16 to be exact) years younger than I was, gorgeous, impeccably dressed, and had a ridiculous smile that made me want to melt. We chatted there for a few minutes until he pulled me over to the bar for a shot. Shit.

We had a couple of drinks, and he started enticing me back to his place for an after party. He said there were tons of people coming over, described where he lived, and so on.

Now, you and I both know there was no such after party at his house. I went along with it though and agreed—happily—to go. As I was finishing my last drink, I had an in-depth, honest conversation with myself: "Heather, you know this guy is just trying to hook up with you, right?" Right. "You know no one else will be at his house, right?" Right. "You know if you go to his house, he'll expect you to have sex with him, right?" Right. "You know if you do have sex with him, you'll probably never hear from him again, right?" Right. "And you're totally okay with that, right?" Right. "You've got enough money for a cab back to your car later, right?" Right. I had answered all these questions for myself and made an adult woman decision to move forward. Just for the record, and despite what you may think based on the stories I've shared, I am not one to go home with strangers. I'm super, super picky, but I was at a crossroads in my life at that exact moment and decided what the hell.

We took a cab to his place, and just as I suspected, the place was empty. I giggled to myself and walked in. It turned out to be an awesome night. We laughed, talked, listened to music, had amazing sex all night, and fell asleep (albeit briefly) together—we had a lot of fun. The next morning I offered to take a cab back to my car, but he insisted on driving me to it, which was nice. When we were almost to my car, I realized he hadn't asked for my number. At this point, I was a little bummed, but not surprised as I'd already told myself this would happen. I was perfectly willing to get out of the car and never see him again. I couldn't remember his name anyway, so there was no way for me stalk him on Facebook, thank God. But just as I was getting out of the car, he asked for my number. Whew. (And that's why I don't go home with strangers. I'll admit the whole thing gave me a little anxiety.)

We ended up hanging out with each other quite a bit over the next couple of months. We went to great happy hours and dinners, shared a lot about ourselves, met each other's friends, talked about taking trips together, had energizing conversations, and had lots of fun. I told all my girlfriends about him, and most of them had met him. I know (and you know by now), this was a mistake, but, hey, I'm human. I got caught up and couldn't help myself.

We were not exclusive, and both of us understood the other was dating around. I remember us talking one night and me telling him our relationship would be enjoyable while it lasted, and when it was over, we'd be friends. And that would be it. I had it in my mind I was going to "control" this relationship down the road of fun and frolic and not make a big deal about it when it was over.

But while I started out with those best of intentions, as it turned out, I really liked this one. With as much dating as I had done, it was still rare for me to come across someone who could get under my skin. It didn't happen often, so when it did, it took extra effort for me to keep my emotions out of it.

We continued to date casually until the day I felt the expected "shift" occur, and The Finale began to pull away from me. I had heightened senses by then and could feel almost immediately when the energy (and the relationship) with him changed.

We had been seeing each other and communicating regularly for just less than two months. One Sunday afternoon he came over, and I cooked us dinner, which is something I rarely do for anyone I am casually dating. It's too personal. But, I gotta tell ya...

this really was a great night. In my mind, it was the best night we had shared thus far. We had a wonderful meal, shared a couple bottles of wine, enjoyed each other's company…it was very easy, very intimate, and it ended in a very positive way.

And it was right after our perfect night he started pulling away. I heard from him once during the next two weeks.

You're wondering why he started pulling away, aren't you? Remember me telling you how guys tend to pull away after super intimate moments? Especially guys who are just casually dating? Well, this wasn't the first time this had happened to me. So I knew exactly what was going on. Remember The Prelude? Same type of thing. Guys aren't assholes for acting this way…it just happens. You can't read into it too much, or you'll drive yourself crazy.

Anyway, he went from texting me every other day to texting me once in two weeks and sporadically thereafter. Whenever he did text me though, it was good. The texts were always sexy and fun, and kept me wanting more. I followed my own rules though and didn't initiate, I only responded. I knew if he wanted to see me, he'd make it happen. He hinted around about getting together, but never actually setup a date. Luckily, I travel for my job and was gone most of November, which made it easier for me not to communicate as much. Then…I got the first "miss you" text while I was away on my trip. Dammit. The "miss you" text always comes when you're trying to pull away, when you haven't communicated for a while, or when you're with another dude. Never fails. Sometimes I think guys throw it out there just to see what kind of response they get. They can sense when you're starting to let go, so they tug on the line just to make sure you're still there. I was.

The Finale's "miss you, you should be here" text came while he was in Vegas on a trip with the boys. A trip we were supposed to go on together…but whatever. Moving on. At this point, I *should* have pulled back drastically because I instinctively knew the relationship had already started coming to an end.

I got back to Phoenix, and the next night he met me out with all my friends. Looking back now, it was that night I knew I was a goner. He was awesome around all my friends, very sweet and accommodating. He took care of everyone. All the girls loved him, which made me fall even harder. I'll admit it's hard not to develop feelings for someone you've spent quality time with, even when you know from the beginning it isn't going to last. If you're casually dating a guy you actually like, there will always come a point in the relationship when you're faced with this situation. You just have to recognize what is happening and make a choice: leave the relationship at that critical point to prevent future hurt feelings and drama, or move forward and risk it. I had no real fear of heartbreak any longer, so I chose to move forward and risk it. And, I'm so glad I did because we had the best "miss you" sex ever that night.

I happened to leave my ID at his house (no, not on purpose), so we made plans to get together Monday evening. Just before we left for dinner, he said, "You know I like having you over, but I like having other girls over, too." I sat there stunned for a minute because this comment had come out of nowhere. I replied, "Uh, okay, that's fine with me," and we left. Unfortunately, that comment was just the beginning of what would end up being a really shitty evening.

From the beginning of our relationship, The Finale had made little jokes here and there about my age, but nothing ever hurt my feelings. I let the comments slide because I'm pretty secure and used to dating younger guys. On this night, however, he made a super derogatory comment about my age and my looks all at the same time, then followed it up shortly thereafter with a dig at my dating savvy…and that hit a cord. I was pissed. And I was hurt. We had just spent this really great night together and now this? I dropped him off at home and swore to myself I'd never see him again. Now mind you, this type of behavior was totally out of character for him, so looking back there must have been something that motivated it. But to be honest, the cause didn't really matter. For whatever reason he felt like he needed to say those things, and I'm pretty sure he knew they'd piss me off. He was pushing me away on purpose.

After that night, again, I tried to pull away from him. I never really told him I was upset—I just stopped communicating as much. Remember the tip about no explanations and no expectations? This is a good example of that. He never asked, and I never said anything. No need to create drama. No need to have the last word. Plus, most of the time, a woman makes up a bunch of shit in her head about how different things are with a guy, while the guy, really, is the same as he's always been. To The Finale, I'm sure nothing was all that different between us. We communicated here and there, flirted here and there, and saw each other here and there whenever it was convenient. All the while I continued to stew about the stupid comment he made that should have rolled off my back but didn't because I was in a heightened state of sensitivity knowing our relationship was slowly coming to an end.

A month passed until we saw each other again. We ended up getting together one night right before the holidays because he was leaving to go home for three weeks. Again, looking back, I pushed for this get together when I should have just wished him a happy holiday over the phone. We had a great night, but leaving the next morning was a little awkward. When he said "Keep in touch" as I walked out the door, I knew I was screwed. That phrase, in any context whatsoever, if coming from a guy, is not good. Now I know I've talked about the various mistakes I made up until this point, but here is where I started making big mistakes…

After our last get together, I truly, truly should have let the relationship go. It could have ended on a high note, and we both would have been just fine. But instead, I reached out to him a couple of times over the holidays (another rule of mine broken). It was wonderful because we had these great chats that

included all the miss yous I was longing to hear...
but not wonderful because it created in my mind a
bond between us that wasn't really there. He was just
being sweet.

He got back home the first week of January, and based
on our conversations over the holiday, I thought for
sure we'd be getting together within a few days. But
one week went by. Two weeks went by. Three weeks
went by. We finally caught each other on FB at the
same time one afternoon, and I decided to push the
issue. I asked him why he hadn't reached out to me.
He said he had made some big decisions during his
time back home and realized he needed to focus on
his work and personal ventures. He said he needed to
stay away from any distractions (aka me). He said he
had been spending a lot of time reflecting on his life
and planning his future. He said he missed me and
would be in touch soon.

Now...who can tell me what this exchange actually
meant? Anyone? Anyone? It meant one of two things.
One, he wasn't interested in me anymore and didn't
want to hurt my feelings. Or two, he was seeing
someone he liked better than me and didn't want to
hurt my feelings. The point is...he was trying to be
nice and not hurt my feelings.

We exchanged a few more texts here and there... but then four weeks went by. We exchanged texts on Valentine's Day (because I started it), but then five weeks went by. Six weeks went by, and we still had no definite plans to see each other. To make a long story even longer, we didn't see each other again until mid-March. Now you'd think by mid-March I would have let go. And mind you, I had a full bench and was dating a bunch, so there was no reason for me to still be pining over this guy.

The night we spent together in March was good, but weird. Things were different between us, and he noticed it, too. After the first kiss of the night he said, "It feels like something has changed." Now despite what you might think about guys, they can sense things. Things had changed. My guard was up because by this point, I was finally following my own advice—trying to end the relationship on a high note and transition him into the Friend Zone. And he, come to find out, had in fact been regularly seeing someone else. For how long I don't know. And honestly, when he told me, I really didn't care because I had already expected to hear it.

When we said goodbye, I knew it would be months before I saw him again, if ever...even though he said he'd call me the next day. I just smiled and kissed him goodnight. I knew it wouldn't take me long to get over him, and eventually I'd get to a place where I might entertain the occasional booty call. But I wasn't there quite yet.

My breakout moment came just a few weeks later. I ran into him where it all began, W Hotel. I noticed him early in the evening but purposefully made a point to not say hello. Of course I kept my eye on him like a hawk though. I don't know exactly when he saw me, but he eventually walked over to talk to me and my friend Lisa. To tell you the truth, I was secretly very excited to see him. My stomach went crazy the moment he touched me. And that smile—I wanted to die. He took us to the bar for shots. The same bar I had seen him at earlier in the night with another set of girls (the irony…I know). After we did our shots we all sat down to relax. He pulled me into his arms, and I swear, I thought I was going to drown from the flood of feelings and emotion running through my body. I wanted to melt right into him, but I knew it would be a huge mistake.

We got up and walked over to the table where his friends were, and it was there in that very moment I made my choice. While he was talking to his friends, I grabbed Lisa and said, "Let's go." It took every ounce of dignity and discipline in my body to walk away from that table. Lisa and I went back to the bar and started chatting with some other guys. The Finale could have interrupted. He could have come and gotten me. But he didn't. I happened to glance over a little while later and saw them all leaving without me. It was like a knife going straight into my gut.

But…

After that, The Finale and I continued to exchanged texts here and there, and we eventually let the relationship transition into a great friendship. We still see each other out and about all the time, and you know what? It's all good. And, I'm happy to report we finally reached booty call status. Like I've said before, a girls gotta keep a good booty call on the bench...

True Bliss...At Last

Well ladies, here we are. True bliss...at last. I hope you received exactly what you needed while taking a trip through my sordid love life, and I hope you've already successfully put some of my tips into action. As you read in my last chapter, mistakes will continue to happen—I can assure you. But don't beat yourself up over it. The trick is recognizing when you're making a mistake and understanding why. One day you'll catch—and stop—yourself before you ever make it. That will be a beautiful day.

And what about that double standard in dating? I think we can all agree it's time to set a new standard—one that allows women to be happy-go-lucky when dating, to date as much and as many people as they want to, and to have sex with whomever the hell they want to, as long as they're sophisticated, smart, and safe about it. Men have been operating this way for centuries. We can, too. No need for a woman to apologize for being someone who knows what she wants and isn't afraid to go after it.

It all boils down to the motto I take with me wherever I go: "Control is Key." Just remember the only person you can control in any situation—you.

19

Quickie list of Dos and Don'ts

I wanted to make it easy on ya, so here's a quick reference guide to what I believe are the most important tips in this book:

- Control is Key! Control yourself and your emotions.

- Don't lose yourself in a guy and forget who you are or what you want.

- Don't settle just to say you're settled down.

- Make the best of casual dating—you'll have to do it at some point.

- Watch yourself: no taking the leap from first date to happily-ever-after.

- There's one common denominator in every relationship: you.

- Dating should not be a husband-hunting adventure.

- Dating is a game, and games take practice.

- Start thinking and dating like a man.

- A great casual relationship is not meant to last forever.

- Jumping head first into dating right after a serious breakup is a big mistake.

- A whirlwind romance is likely to turn into a tornado.

- Any woman can lose her mind over a guy. Any woman.

- When the relationship ends, move on.

- Have enough self-respect to walk away from a bad situation.

- Always carry $100 in cash just in case you need to bail your friend out of a "throwing keys" situation.

- Not learning from your mistakes is the biggest mistake of all.

- The worst thing you can do is date one guy at a time.

- Build your bench, and always keep it fresh with new players.

- Casual dating teaches you how to create boundaries and value you.

- Trust your instincts. If you smell a rat, then don't offer up the cheese.

- Be fun, flirty, and flexible.

- There are no expectations in casual dating. No exceptions.

- Always have a backup plan.

- Start with the end in mind.

- Limit the time you spend with a guy—not more than two days a week, never two nights in a row, etc.

- Be cautious about bringing bench guys around friends and family.

- Don't let drugs and alcohol create feelings that aren't real.

- Don't blow off friends at the last minute or change your plans to accommodate a guy's schedule.

- If you're going to play the game, be prepared to take some hits.

- The one who cares the least has the most power.

- If he wants to go out with you, he will find you.

- Don't take your feelings too seriously.

- Never give respect to a guy who doesn't respect you.

- Look at every relationship as an opportunity.

- Just chill!!

- Always have a plan to keep from getting stranded.

- Don't post pics of you with any guy you're dating on any social media site.

- Don't be interested in him just because he's interested in you.

- Be careful that with weekend getaways your emotions are not what get away.

- Don't reveal too much about yourself.

- Holidays are for loved ones and friends.

- Keep your emotions under control at all times around guys.

- Recognize your pattern; then break it.

- You don't owe him any explanations, for anything.

- Don't expect any explanations from him, for anything.

- Live your life for you, not for a man.

- Don't give more than you get.

- The honeymoon is over when you start "working" on your casual relationship.

- If you don't like the ride, get off.

- You've spent some time together, had some fun and great sex—that's it.

- If your friends can see right through him, so should you.

- Trust yourself to walk away from the wrong guy.

- Lick your wounds and move on.

- Don't make a guy turn into super jerk.

- Don't worry about getting closure. If he stops calling, it's closed.

- Be that powerful woman who doesn't have to prove herself.

- Red flags don't go away—they multiply.

- Don't confuse infatuation with love.

- Most guys don't set out to be jerks.

- When you see him start to break his pattern of behavior, start preparing for the end.

- Know what your boundaries are, and don't cross them for any man.

- Always keep your dignity in mind—and intact.

- Watch out for signs you need an intervention.

- No man is worth losing yourself or your friends over.

- There's no need to get the last word.

- Learn to love being alone!

20

Quickies About Sex

Like I've said before...sex when you're casually dating is a very personal decision. I know lots of women who have no problem with casual sex, and I know lots of women who realize they get too emotionally attached and can't do it. To each her own. Personally, it took me some time to separate sex from love because that's how I was raised. As we've learned though, casual relationships aren't usually about love. They are about fun, excitement, and exploration. I've learned to enjoy casual sex when the scenario is right for me. You need to decide what's right for you. Here are some quick tips for you to keep in mind:

- If you want to have sex with a guy, do it. Just know you may never hear from him again.

- If you have sex with a guy and never hear from him again, don't call or text him. Save your dignity. He got what he wanted (and maybe you did, too), now move on. If he wants to see you again, he will contact you.

- If you have sex with a guy, and he calls you for another rendezvous, don't assume it will go any further. It just means he likes you enough to have sex with you one more time.

- You've heard the saying, "The best way to get over one man is to get under another." Well, that plan works great, but it can also backfire. Make sure you're doing it for the right reason, and only you know what that reason is. Personally, I'm a fan of recycling someone on the bench. You already know the guy, you know the sex will be good, you know he won't get weird on you. You know you won't fall in love with him. Overall, it's a good solution to help kick-start your recovery.

- Never tell a guy how much you love (or use) your vibrator. It will only make him feel like he has to "make" you stop using it. If you're lucky enough to find a guy who welcomes your guest, then make sure he knows you appreciate him more because guys like that don't come 'round that often.

- There are so many rules out there about sex. Make him wait if you're really interested. Don't have sex on the first date. You're a worthless slut if you sleep with more than one guy at a time. Rules about sex don't really apply in today's day and age and certainly don't apply in casual dating. I know so many couples who slept together on the first night and have been together since, blissfully happy and married with children. Do what feels right. You know yourself better than anyone else. Just know the possible consequences, and be ready to deal with them if they arise.

- There is no reason for you to spend the night with a guy unless you plan to have sex.

- Limit the snuggling to only when you are watching a movie. Snuggling after sex is a little too intimate for casual dating.

- Bring your own protection. It cracks me up when a guy says, "I don't have anything," and I say, "You're in luck...I do." As if. Like my friend Stacey says…"This is a recreational area – not a factory". Love it!

- Just because you planned to spend the night doesn't mean you have to. Don't feel bad about leaving after sex. Just tell him you decided to go home.

- Don't have sex with a man unless you are absolutely certain it will not affect you emotionally. If you're the type of woman who gets attached, don't fool yourself into thinking you can have sex without getting attached. You can't. Some women are able to separate the two, some aren't. Know which one you are.

- Every girl needs a friend who can pick her up at 4 a.m. because you do not want to spend the night with a hookup. Sometimes these situations end well, and sometimes they don't. At a minimum, you should always have enough money in your purse to get a cab back to your car or house, or have enough money in your bank account to get a hotel room for a night.

- If you can't trust him to call when he says he will, or show up when he's supposed to, how can you trust him enough to have sex with him? I get that casual sex isn't really about trust, but it doesn't have to be about anxiety and irritation either.

- In casual relationships, once you start having sex, you really can't stop. It's not cool for you to withhold sex and play games to get what you want. This is a "casual" relationship. It's supposed to be fun. If it's gotten to this point, he should dump you.

- Threesomes are fun, but you have to handle yourself appropriately. If you're the addition to a couple, make sure it's all about her and not him. If it's three individuals with no ties, do whatever the heck you want.

- Having sex with "friends" can be tricky, especially if it's a group of friends who hang out together a lot. The friendship has to be really solid for sex not to shake it or rattle the group dynamic.

- Stay away from sleeping with more than one guy in the same friend group. Pick one, and stick with him. Then move on to another group. You really don't want to be *that* girl.

- If you've just had sex with a guy and you're getting ready to leave (or he's leaving), and he makes no attempt to setup the next communication or meeting with you (*e.g.*, "Can I get your number?" "I'll call you tomorrow." "What are you doing next week?" "That was awesome—I can't wait to do it again!"), assume you'll never see him again. If you do, it's a bonus. If he's just now asking what your name is, you're screwed. Just turn around and walk out.

- Understand that most women are wired to connect sex with love. Understand that most men are wired to connect sex with sex.

- For most women, having sex too early in a relationship tends to intensify feelings that aren't real.

- It gets tricky when a guy you're casually dating is super intimate and tender with you in bed. Don't get me wrong. It's nice. But it's a Danger Zone for sure. It's really hard when he's throwing out "I love you" and shit when you've only been seeing each other a couple of months. We all know those words mean nothing in the heat of the moment, but those little words will creep into your brain and pitch a tent. It will irritate the hell out of you, and you'll secretly look forward to it happening again.

- It's socially acceptable for men to date around and have multiple sex partners. It's still not socially acceptable for women.

- Society can suck it.

21

Acknowledgements

A. Justin Sterling & the Sterling Institute of Relationship

Back in 2000 I attended a weekend event that changed my life forever. It's called the Sterling Women's Weekend. The purpose of the Sterling Women's Weekend is to engage in the process of locating the source of your power, and discovering and dissolving the barriers between you, and manifesting that power in your relationships, and in the world. After this weekend I spent the next 10 years studying the discipline of all relationships, and it was during this time I found my power, my voice, and peace within myself. Because of the Sterling Women's Weekend, I also found the strength to execute my dream of publishing this book. I will be forever grateful to the countless number of Sterling women and men in my life who have loved and supported me along this journey. Thank you.

Jennifer Pillen Banks, CrossDot Writing Solutions, LLC

Since I started this process, I've been presented with the perfect person at the perfect time, and

Jennifer was no exception. I was looking for an editor, and Jennifer was introduced to me through my friend Michael Sinkula at AlphaGraphics. Jennifer and I met for happy hour one afternoon to see if we were a good fit for each other, and I've been in heaven since. She has made this book so much richer than I could have ever hoped for. Thank you Jennifer for helping my true voice be heard.

Michael Sinkula, and the team at AlphaGraphics

When I decided to move forward with finishing this book, Michael was the first person who reached out to help. He kept after me, and followed up with me, and kept after me, and followed up with me, until I finally took the leap. He made the whole process a lot less scary for me and patiently guided me every step of the way. The team at AlphaGraphics has been amazing to work with and has helped bring all my ideas to life. Thank you Michael for sticking with me and making this actually happen!

Andrew Pielage, AP Photography

Words cannot express how much I adore and admire Andy. His friendship and inspiration through this process brought me over the finish line with my hands held high. His unique vision, ideas, and flawless photographs have transformed me into a person I'm proud to present to the world. Thank you so much Andy—I am forever grateful.

Renee Towell, RT Public Relations

Renee was the very first person I reached out to when I had nothing but a few ideas on paper. She spent a year coaching me and helping me develop my image, get comfortable with it, design my website, and sharpen my writing skills. She pushed me beyond my comfort zone, and I am truly thankful for everything she did for me. Thank you, Renee.

And…to Jason Tietjen, thank you for all your support and great ideas, and for kicking my butt so I would take the first step.

To Deanine Mancini and Lisa Turley, many thanks for making me look so fabulous swinging a sledge hammer and for your contributions to the final title of this book.

To all the awesome guys who played a part in the making of this movie (ha ha) and who will now and forever more remain nameless—thank you!

And finally, thank you to a small select group of my kick-ass friends who made big contributions to this venture. As Clarice would say, I love each and every one of you more than my luggage. In no particular order...Kate Good, Stephanie Davis, Stacey Schlessinger, Melissa Foley, Jennifer Daly, Jean Herges, Darlesa Buckalew, Claudine Song, Jennifer Stamp, and Chris Stella.